D0490082

175 YEARS OF
CUNARD

175 YEARS OF CUNARD

CHRIS FRAME & RACHELLE CROSS

FOREWORD BY STEPHEN M. PAYNE, OBE, DESIGNER OF QM2
WITH STORIES FROM CUNARD CAPTAINS, CREW AND GUESTS

The
History
Press

For Zac

387.5065461
FRA.

Cover images: *front*: *QM2* berthed at Laem Chebang during her 2009 world cruise
(Author's collection), *back*: *QE2* and *Queen Victoria* in Sydney harbour in 2008 (Cunard/
Michael Gallagher), *back flap, top*: *QE2*'s Queens Room (Cunard/Michael Gallagher),
middle: helicopter departing from *QE2* (R.W. Warwick; *QE2*: The Cunard Flagship
Queen Elizabeth II collection), *bottom*: Cunard Three Queens postcard (Marc-Antoine
Bombail/Ocean Books)
The image on page 2 is *QE2*, *Queen Victoria* and *QM2* in Southampton in 2008. (Cunard/
Michael Gallagher)

First published 2015

The History Press
The Mill, Brimscombe Port
Stroud, Gloucestershire, GL5 2QG
www.thehistorypress.co.uk

© Chris Frame and Rachelle Cross, 2015

The right of Chris Frame and Rachelle Cross to be identified as the Authors
of this work has been asserted in accordance with the Copyright, Designs and
Patents Act 1988.

British Library Cataloguing in Publication Data.
A catalogue record for this book is available from the British Library.

ISBN 978 0 7524 8926 1

Typesetting and origination by The History Press
Printed in India

CONTENTS

FOREWORD

by Stephen M. Payne, OBE RDI

Cunard Line 1840–2015

Many organisations can trace their origins back 100 years but the venerable Cunard Line can better that by a considerable margin; 2015 marks 175 years of transoceanic service by the enterprise, which was founded by Samuel Cunard to ferry passengers and mail from the old world to the new and back again.

During this time the world has changed enormously. As the Industrial Revolution gathered pace in the nineteenth century, populations found new freedoms in mobility. The railways played a major part in this development and it was only natural that technical advances first used on land should eventually be deployed at sea. Steam propulsion supplied the means to provide a reliable service that sail alone could not offer. It was Samuel Cunard, aided by a British Government Royal Mail contract, that took this ideal to a logical conclusion and built four diminutive paddle steamers that could offer a regular, scheduled service. Since Cunard's first ship, *Britannia*, set forth across the Atlantic on 4 July 1840, Cunard has remained true to its roots and maintained an Atlantic presence; only during the two world wars were services suspended.

Cunard ships embraced continuous technological advancement as wooden paddle steamers like *Britannia* gave way to iron-hulled paddlers, such as the record-breaking *Persia* of 1855; paddles gave way to screw propellers from *China* (1862) onwards and iron gave way to steel with *Servia* in 1881. As the ships grew in size and speed increased, steam reciprocating machinery gave way to steam turbine, which latterly has been supplanted by diesels and gas turbines.

Many of the greatest ships in the world have been Cunarders. The epoch-making *Lusitania* and *Mauretania* (1907) pushed the technologies of the day to new heights to secure Cunard's supremacy on the Atlantic following challenges from continental Europe and America. During the heady era of grand 'ships of state' in the late 1920s and 1930s, only the mighty *Queen Mary* turned a profit without the aid of government subsidy. Subsequent Queens, *Elizabeth* (1940) and *Elizabeth 2* (1969), utilised advances in marine engineering and naval architecture to represent the pinnacle of the shipbuilders' art. Latterly, Cunard's present-day Queens are the benchmark for efficiency and modernity.

Apart from being the flag bearer for the British merchant marine on the North Atlantic, Cunard has rendered invaluable service in ferrying troops around the world in times of conflict. The first such occurrence was in 1854, when fourteen Cunard ships were requisitioned for government service to the Crimea. During the First World War, Cunard ships were employed as troop transports, hospital ships and as armed merchant cruisers. Losses in both ships and personnel were inevitably severe. The Second World War saw a repeat of the first, with Cunard ships at the vanguard. At the end of the war, Sir Winston Churchill, Britain's wartime prime minister, concluded that Cunard's *Queen Mary* and *Queen Elizabeth* had shortened the conflict by a year due to their enormous capacity, which allowed the rapid movement of large numbers of troops across oceanic divides. In a later conflict, the Falklands War (1982), it was Cunard's *Queen Elizabeth 2* that ferried the largest troop contingent down to the South Atlantic.

In January 1923, *Laconia* (1922) embarked on the company's first world cruise that lasted over four months, visiting twenty-two ports. This celebrated voyage was such a success that it was repeated the following year. The Great Depression of the 1930s left Cunard with ships but few passengers wishing to use its traditional services. Cunard took to cruising to fill its express liners between transatlantic voyages, the short prohibition-busting 'booze cruises' proving a popular diversion for thirsty Americans. In 1949, the superlative *Caronia*, dubbed the 'Green Goddess' due to her green paint scheme, entered Cunard service as the most luxurious cruise liner in the world. The traditions embraced by Cunard and epitomised by *Caronia* are perpetuated today with the present-day Queens – *Mary 2*, *Victoria* and *Elizabeth*.

Whilst a company can build great ships and offer routes and services, success can only be ensured by the people that provide the human touch: the crew. Indeed, it is often said that a ship is only as good as its crew. Cunard has been renowned for the service provided by its crews. Today, in deference to when White Star Line merged with Cunard in 1934, the service standard on board Cunard ships is termed 'White Star Service'. At a time when company loyalty is not as in the past, many Cunard crew members eschew the trend and choose to remain with the company. Thus, the new Queens resonate with stories from *Queen Elizabeth 2* and other Cunarders, and are so much the richer for it.

This book is a celebration of great enterprise, of service and of people. Cunard is a very special company with a rich and varied past – and a bright future. The Blue Peter is flying and the whistle has sounded and soon we'll be casting off. So come on board as we set sail on this voyage of discovery.

Stephen M. Payne, OBE RDI
Designer Queen Mary 2

ACKNOWLEDGEMENTS

We would like to thank everyone who has helped us to share the story of Cunard over the last 175 years.

Our thanks go to Stephen Payne for writing such a fitting foreword for the book. Stephen has been so instrumental in securing the future of Cunard Line since he designed *QM2*, and his words are a tribute to both Cunard's past and its future.

Thank you also to Ann Sherry, CEO of Carnival Australia, for her words about the significance of Cunard's 175th anniversary in the afterword of this book.

Thank you to all those who provided us with quotes and stories, including Barry Brown, Anthony Davis, Jamie Firth, Alastair Greener, Christel Hansen, Eli Iniesta, Rob Lightbody, Elaine Mackay, Captain McNaught, Bill Miller, Andrew Olliviere, Carmel Rogers, Commodore Rynd, Caroline Scallan, Gaynor van Deventer, Commodore R.W. Warwick and Sam Warwick.

We are also very grateful to the photographers, collectors and historians who shared photographic content with us for this book.

Once again we send our heartfelt thanks to Ian Boyle for allowing us use of some of his extensive collection of maritime postcards and photographs. We are highly impressed by his collection, some of which can be found at www.simplonpc.co.uk.

Cunard's legendary *Queen Mary* departs Southampton. (Colin Hargreaves)

We are likewise grateful to maritime historians Rob Henderson and Doug Cremer for access to their impressive Cunard and White Star Line collection used in this book.

Our thanks to Michael Pocock, of Maritime Quest, for the use of his collection. Michael's impressive archive of photographs can be seen at www.maritimequest.com.

We are also grateful to photographer Nick Souza who gave us access to the brilliant photographs of QM2 meeting Queen Mary.

Further thanks and acknowledgement goes to Tee Adams, Marc-Antoine Bombail, Ian Boyle, Robin Burn, Ross Burnside, Thad Constantine, Doug Cremer, Andy Fitzsimmons, George Frame, Jan Frame, Michael Gallagher, Colin Hargreaves, Rob Henderson, Pam Massey, Bill Miller, Frank X. Prudent, Andrew Sassoli-Walker, Russell Smith, Nick Souza, Commodore R.W. Warwick and Cunard Line, all of whom assisted us with imagery.

And finally, many thanks to our commissioning editor, Amy Rigg, managing editor, Juanita Zoë Hall, and designer, Glad Stockdale.

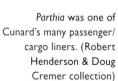

Parthia was one of Cunard's many passenger/ cargo liners. (Robert Henderson & Doug Cremer collection)

1

THE COMPANY'S BEGINNINGS

Three cheers more and as the first one rings upon our ears the vessel throbs like a strong giant that has just received the breath of life; the two great wheels turn fiercely round for the first time; and the noble ship, with wind and tide astern, breaks proudly through the lashed and foamy water.

Charles Dickens writing of his voyage aboard RMS Britannia *in* American Notes

The first official voyage of the Cunard Line departed Liverpool on 4 July 1840. The ship was the RMS *Britannia* and her crossing to Boston, via Halifax, ushered in a new era in transatlantic shipping. *Britannia* was the first in a quartet of steam-powered paddle steamers built for the Cunard Line and commenced what was to be the first regular transatlantic passenger and mail steam service.

The Cunard Line was originally known as the British & North American Royal Mail Steam Packet Company and was started by the Halifax, Nova Scotia, businessman Samuel Cunard in partnership with Scottish businessmen George and James Burns, David and Charles McIver and Robert Napier. The company was created to operate a mail service between Britain and North America, after Samuel Cunard successfully tendered for the British Government's mail contract.

In the early part of the nineteenth century a mail contract was very lucrative for shipping companies. The contract provided the company with a steady source of income and many of the shipping companies that started around this time relied on the government contract for financial stability. The mail contracts allowed companies to establish a sea route, which could then be expanded to include additional services, such as passenger and cargo transportation.

The British Government had called for tenders for a steamship-operated transatlantic mail service in November 1838, and in 1839 Samuel Cunard travelled to Great Britain to make his bid for the service. On the recommendation of an associate, he engaged the services of Robert Napier, a Scottish shipbuilder, who introduced him to his other future business partners. Napier also worked on the design and build of the first four vessels, which would allow Cunard to complete the requirements of the mail contract.

Britannia was the first of the quartet. At 207ft long, she was a wooden-hulled paddle steamer. The paddle wheels and their machinery took up the majority of the space on board amidships. The cargo hold occupied most of the rest of the space, but, Samuel Cunard, seeing the possibilities, had also instructed builders Robert Duncan & Co. to include passenger accommodation, thus *Britannia* could accommodate up to 115 passengers in a single class.

The accommodation aboard *Britannia* was far from luxurious. Passenger spaces were limited and basic in their design, as per Cunard's instruction: 'I want a plain and comfortable boat, not the least unnecessary expense for show. I prefer plain work in the cabin, and it will save a large amount in the cost.'

As such, passengers slept in bunks, entertained themselves and ate food that was prepared from preserved and dried stores or sourced from the chickens and a cow carried aboard.

Author Charles Dickens, who travelled aboard *Britannia*, described his first view of the ship's grand saloon as a 'long narrow apartment not unlike a gigantic hearse with windows in the sides, having at the upper end a melancholy stove at which three or four chilly stewards were warming their hands'.

Despite these discomforts, *Britannia* represented a huge step forward for the travelling passenger. Prior to *Britannia* there were few steam ships operating on the North Atlantic. Those that did offer a service, such as Brunel's *Great Western*, offered services in isolation, meaning that the voyages, while scheduled, were not based around a regular timetable (such as a fortnightly sailing).

The other option for those wishing to cross the North Atlantic was to take a journey by sailing packet. Being reliant on wind power made the sailing journey inherently unreliable; there was no way to guarantee the sailing time and thus it was extremely difficult for shipping companies operating sailing packets to provide a regular service.

This all changed, however, once *Britannia* and her three sister ships, *Acadia*, *Caledonia* and *Columbia*, were in service. With each of these ships

▶ **DID YOU KNOW?**

In March 1849, *Britannia* was sold to the German Confederation Navy and renamed *Barbarossa*. She was later transferred to the Prussian Navy and, in 1880, was sunk whilst being used as a target ship.

Britannia was the first Cunarder; here she is depicted aboard *QM2*'s 'Maritime Quest'. (Pam Massey)

having a maximum speed of 9 knots and an average crossing time of fourteen days, Cunard was able to offer a regular schedule, with a ship departing Liverpool once a fortnight.

This made the sending of mails much faster, easier and more reliable. The mail contract had specified the speed the ships needed to make and also the timings of the sailings to be made. If Cunard failed to adhere to these schedules hefty fines were imposed, regardless of whether the company was at fault or not.

Despite the financial implications of any delays, Cunard insisted on a policy of safety over speed with Samuel Cunard giving his captains simple instructions: '... ship, passengers and mail – bring them safely over and safely back'. This policy was to stand the company in good stead for the future.

The Cunard service quickly proved popular and it was not long before Cunard had commissioned a further two ships. The *Hibernia* and the *Cambria* were slightly bigger and faster than the original four ships and held the speed records for their Atlantic crossings. At 219ft long and 35ft wide, they each had the capacity to carry 120 passengers per voyage.

In spite of their safety policy, the Cunard ships were not able to completely avoid the perils of the sea. On 2 July 1843, the Cunarder *Columbia* ran aground in thick fog off the coast of Seal Island. Although the ship subsequently broke up, she was successfully evacuated with no loss of life.

In 1847, the mail contract was renegotiated and the government requested that Cunard increase the number of sailings to have a ship depart once a week from Liverpool, bound for Boston or Canada.

▶ **DID YOU KNOW?** . . . .

Prior to *Britannia* entering service, the steamship *Unicorn* was sent across the Atlantic to Boston by Samuel Cunard. This had the joint effect of creating interest in the new Cunard services, as well as repositioning the *Unicorn*, which was to run a feeder service between Boston and Canada.

Sails were gradually superseded by steam engines. (Authors' collection)

The new contract was signed and four new ships were built, *Europa*, *America*, *Canada* and *Niagara*.

At over 1,820 tons each and carrying 140 first-class passengers, these ships were both larger and faster than their predecessors. They were also the first ships to use signal lights at night to assist with safe navigation. A red light on the port side, green on the starboard meant that even at night other ships could tell in which direction the Cunarders were travelling. This innovation is still used aboard ships today.

The new quartet was also capable of carrying guns in times of war. The requirement to be able to carry guns was a stipulation of the mail contracts and signified the government's intent to requisition the ships should the need arise. This was to take effect in 1854 with the outbreak of the Crimean War.

WELCOME ABOARD
QUEEN MARY 2

Eli Iniesta, Cunard Voyage Sales Specialist, shares why she loves Cunard:

I could say that Cunard has given me 'the world', in all senses. Joining Cunard in 2005 completely changed and enriched my life and gave me the best experiences and memories, which will stay with me forever.

It educated me and made me more open and understanding to others. Not least, I got to meet so many people from all around the world, and some of them became real friends for life.

It's probably one of the best things that has happened to me. Maybe I'm brainwashed after nine years, but it makes me very proud to say I work for Cunard, one of the most famous lines in the world.

▶ DID YOU KNOW?

Sir Samuel Cunard preferred paddle-driven ships to those with screw propellers. He considered them to be safer looking and believed passengers preferred them.

Sir Samuel Cunard, as depicted aboard *QM2*. (Pam Massey)

Sir Samuel Cunard and the early Cunard steamers depicted aboard *QE2*. (Authors' collection)

Cunard sailing schedule for the 1841 season. (Robert Henderson & Doug Cremer collection)

SIR SAMUEL CUNARD

Born in Halifax, Canada, on 21 November 1787, Samuel Cunard was the second of nine children. The son of Abraham and Margaret Cunard, Samuel was an exceptionally bright child, displaying high levels of initiative, motivation and entrepreneurship.

Although best known as the founder of the Cunard Line, he had been instrumental in the development and utilisation of steam ships for years before *Britannia* ever took to sea. Samuel married Susan Duffus on 4 February 1815, and together they had nine children of their own. His wife passed away in 1828 and Sir Samuel never remarried.

He was created a baronet by HM Queen Victoria in 1859 for his services to the country, particularly through the Cunard Line and the fleet's invaluable role during both peacetime and war.

After his retirement in 1863, he was succeeded as the head of Cunard Line by his son, Sir Edward, who also succeeded him in the baronetcy. Sir Samuel travelled to Halifax for the final time in the autumn of 1864 aboard the Cunard liner *Scotia*, the last of his paddle-driven transatlantic liners.

On returning to England, his health deteriorated and Sir Samuel died in Kensington on 28 April 1865.

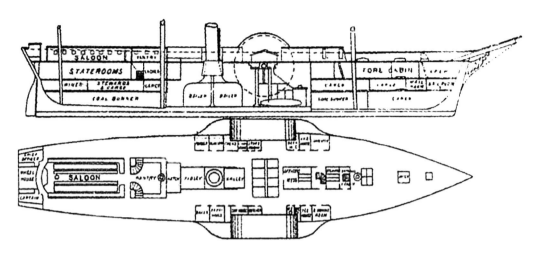

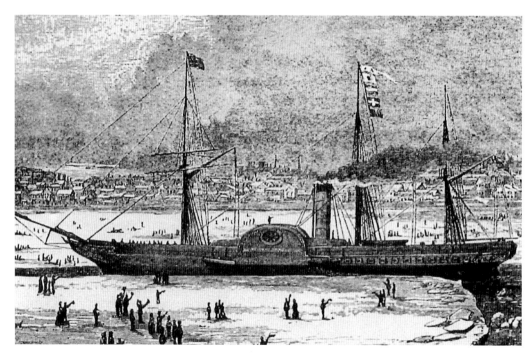

Above: Sir Samuel Cunard, founder of the Cunard Line. (R.W. Warwick; *QE2*: The Cunard Line Flagship Queen Elizabeth II collection)

Above right: Deck plans of Cunard's first ship, *Britannia*. (R.W. Warwick; *QE2*: The Cunard Line Flagship Queen Elizabeth II collection)

Right: Bostonians free *Britannia* from the ice using pickaxes and shovels. (R.W. Warwick; *QE2*: The Cunard Line Flagship Queen Elizabeth II collection)

▶ **DID YOU KNOW?**

RMS stands for Royal Mail Ship.

2

THE EARLY YEARS

The Collins people are pretty much in the situation of finding that breaking our windows with sovereigns, though very fine fun, is too costly to keep on.

Charles McIver to Samuel Cunard

With the advent of the Crimean War, most of the Cunard fleet was requisitioned for war duties, which left the field open for new competitors to grow their own transatlantic shipping companies.

One such company to begin services was the Collins Line. Headed by Edward Knight Collins, the Collins Line commenced North Atlantic steamship services on 27 April 1850 with their 3,000-ton ship *Atlantic*. The Collins Line had obtained a mail subsidy from the American Government on ten-year terms. The subsidy was considerably more lucrative than what was offered to Cunard.

Collins was able to build larger and faster ships that offered far greater luxury than that of the Cunard ships. In addition, he made it a policy for his ships to be as fast as possible. Running the ships at high speed, however, resulted in several problems for the Collins Line; it used more fuel and the increased vibrations led to damage to the vessel, requiring costly repairs.

In response to the competition of Collins Line, Cunard built *Persia* in 1855, their first iron-hulled steamer. *Persia* was able to run at higher speeds, using more powerful engines than any of the previous Cunarders, due to her iron hull. She took both the eastbound and westbound Atlantic speed records from their American rivals in 1856.

Collins Line was not to remain a threat to Cunard for long as a number of disasters ultimately led to the folding of the company. The first such disaster occurred in September 1854, when their ship, *Arctic*, was sunk within 15 miles of the coast after striking another ship in heavy fog. What made this even more tragic for Edward Knight Collins was that his wife, daughter and youngest son were all travelling aboard and were lost with the ship. In 1856, the Collins Line was beset with another tragedy when their ship *Pacific* disappeared during a crossing with all hands.

Despite building a bigger and more luxurious ship, *Adriatic*, to compete for the transatlantic passenger trade, the Collins Line was ultimately unprofitable and was unable to survive the reduction in their government mail contract in 1858.

Throughout Europe there were other new shipping companies opening up, providing continental Europe with steamship connections. Germany was a particular threat, with Hamburg-Amerika Line commencing services in 1847 and Norddeutscher Lloyd establishing Atlantic steam ship services in 1857. With the formation of the German Empire these shipping lines became increasingly aggressive in their expansion of transatlantic services.

The British Inman Line had been started in 1850 and although the line did not have a mail contract in the early years, their revolutionary ship, *City of Glasgow*, was designed specifically to undertake voyages in an economical manner. To achieve this, the ship was completed with an all-iron hull and used the more efficient screw-propeller, rather than paddle wheels, making her cheaper to run and maintain.

Cunard responded to the various challenging lines by building new ships. In 1862, *Scotia* entered service. *Scotia* was to be the last of Cunard's record-breakers to be built with paddle wheels. She had an iron hull and was built on similar lines to their ship *Persia*, from whom she took the speed records, but on a larger scale.

▶ **DID YOU KNOW?**
· ·

Prior to *Servia*, it was widely believed that it was too dangerous to use electricity aboard ships.

Edward Knight Collins was one of Cunard's earliest rivals. (R.W. Warwick; *QE2: The Cunard Line Flagship Queen Elizabeth II* collection)

Britannia was a twin-paddle, steam-powered vessel. (Robert Henderson & Doug Cremer collection)

Film historian Barry Brown was a regular lecturer aboard the Cunard fleet, having spoken on all of the modern Queens as well as Caronia:

As a film historian, I lectured from 2001 to 2012 on *QE2, Caronia, QM2, Queen Victoria* and *Queen Elizabeth*, visiting many interesting countries but, as I live in London, I sailed mostly from Southampton. Ah, such fond memories.

On *QE2* one sunny morning at sea, on-board guests were gathering in the ship's cinema for my 11.15 a.m. lecture on 'The Life and Career of Hollywood's Leading Lady – Bette Davis', whom I had met twice as a BBC TV producer of cinema programmes. At 11.10 a.m. the captain made an announcement that, although the ship was not due to dock in Gibraltar until 12.30 p.m., there was a magnificent view of the island right now from the promenade deck. I'm grateful to those five people who stayed to hear my lecture!

In October 2008, I accepted an offer to lecture on *QM2* from Southampton–New York–Southampton (twelve days) – little did I know that it coincided with the final transatlantic crossings of *QE2*. For hours and hours, I watched the smaller *QE2* sailing in tandem with *QM2*, only 1 mile apart. One day it would sail on the port side of *QM2*, the next day on the starboard side, elegant and graceful. It was joyous to watch this old liner glide across the Atlantic Ocean. The return voyage, both ships departed together from New York, was memorable as *QE2* was given a tremendous send-off. I must have been the only traveller who had boarded the ship unaware of the forthcoming historic event.

My favourite lecture venue on any ship is the 'Illuminations Theatre' on *QM2*, seating 500, each with a good view of the stage. For me to stand, talking to a packed audience with standing-room only was quite thrilling, especially the rapturous applause at the end. It wasn't like that every time but when it did occur, the adrenaline rush was overwhelming. However, jet lag can sometimes be a problem after a long flight to join the ship. On one occasion, I had invited my Australian cousin Christopher to join me on the Sydney-Hong Kong leg of *QM2*'s 2011 world voyage. My lecture on the Australian-born film star Errol Flynn was scheduled for 3.30 p.m. in the Illuminations Theatre. After lunch I decided to have a short nap before getting dressed for my lecture, so my cousin went on deck to catch some sun. He returned to the stateroom at 3.05 p.m. to find me in a very deep sleep. I have never given such a slow, dreary lecture in my life. I wonder if the audience noticed because the positive reception I received was, to my mind, unwarranted.

On the small 24,000-ton *Caronia* I visited the Faroe Islands and Iceland's capital Reykjavik for the first time, two unique ports of call. Another unique feature on *Caronia* was the classless one-sitting-only dining room, so unlike the current Cunard fleet.

My first lecture on *Queen Victoria*, in 2008, was a revelation because the stunning Royal Court Theatre, where the lectures were held, was a replica of a Victorian theatre on the Isle of Man. The technical facilities were excellent and the well-trained crew was reliable and helpful. It was a joy. I lectured on this magnificent ship regularly until April 2011, when I went on a nostalgic Mediterranean voyage to Venice.

In October 2010, I felt honoured to be invited as a lecturer on the maiden voyage of the latest addition to the Cunard fleet, *Queen Elizabeth*. I was chuffed when I gave the first ever lecture on this wonderful vessel, more or less a replica of *Queen Victoria* but with an art deco decor.

My final voyage with Cunard was on *Queen Elizabeth*, from Southampton to Athens, in September 2012. I had been diagnosed with Parkinson's disease, I was 82 years old and I knew it was time to stop. I could not have ended my career on a better ship. I gave six movie lectures, the final one being 'Hollywood's British Gentleman – David Niven'. It was the best of all, just like Cunard.

The Cunard Line crest is still in use after 175 years. (Robert Henderson & Doug Cremer collection)

Collins Line's *Atlantic* was larger than its Cunard counterparts. (R.W. Warwick; *QE2: The Cunard Line Flagship Queen Elizabeth II* collection)

Also entering into service in 1862 was Cunard's *China*. *China* was the first single-screw ship built for the Cunard Line. She was built by Robert Napier & Sons in Scotland and began service on the Liverpool–New York route in March 1862. This ship was unique among the Cunarders at the time of her introduction, in that she was the first to be built with steerage passengers in mind. Steerage accommodation became extremely important throughout the latter part of the nineteenth and early twentieth century. Immigration from Europe to the United States of America was a significant source of income for shipping lines, with millions of people moved by the transatlantic liners during this period.

► **DID YOU KNOW?** . . . .
. . . .

During her maiden voyage in 1883, Cunard's *Aurania* suffered a major incident when her engines exploded. Fortunately there was no loss of life.

In 1871, the first ship for the White Star Line, the *Oceanic*, entered service. *Oceanic* ushered in a new era of steamship design; with her lavish first-class accommodation placed amidships, to reduce movement, she offered passengers a level of comfort not previously seen on the Atlantic.

White Star Line, the brainchild of Thomas Ismay, grew rapidly. A series of agreements saw the line provided with ample capital and the exclusive use of the Harland & Wolff shipyard in Belfast, which meant that White Star ships were built in record times, at cost plus a fixed percentage. Such lucrative terms were not available to the Cunard Line.

The year 1871 also saw the American Line commence operations, and the Inman Line introduce a new liner, *City of Brussels*, which eclipsed *Scotia* to become the fastest ship on the North Atlantic.

In response, Cunard built new tonnage and integrated a series of innovations into their fleet. To this end, Cunard's 1874-built *Bothnia* and her sister ship *Scythia* introduced the first dedicated ladies-only lounge, an on-board library and an indoor smoking room. *Bothnia* and *Scythia* were also the first transatlantic liners to use electric bells, used by first-class passengers to summon their cabin attendant.

In 1876, the mail contracts expired and the new contracts were awarded. Cunard now held only one mail contract, with the others going to Inman Line, Norddeutscher Lloyd and Hamburg-Amerika Lines. To raise capital in the new operating environment, the company reorganised as a publicly listed company in 1879 and was officially renamed as the Cunard Steamship Company Ltd.

In 1881, Cunard was able to launch their first steel-hulled steamship, the *Servia*. *Servia* was the largest ship in service at the time, and second only to the by now retired *Great Eastern*. *Servia* was followed by three iron-hulled vessels, the *Catalonia*, *Pavonia* and *Cephalonia*. These three ships each included accommodation for 200 first-class passengers and 1,500 third-class passengers as well as having the ability to carry cargo.

Passage by steam ship in those early years was sometimes dangerous. (R.W. Warwick; QE2: The Cunard Line Flagship Queen Elizabeth II collection)

John Langley, QC, is the chairman of the Cunard Steamship Society:

Shipping lines have come and gone over the past few centuries … longevity was not a common characteristic … many foundered in a comparatively short period of time, often as a result of horrific losses of ships and passengers on the transatlantic crossing.

Cunard Line is the exception. One hundred and seventy-five years after its founding by Halifax native Samuel Cunard, his company is still making history on the North Atlantic and around the world. Its incomparable record of safety and seamanship remains intact, never to be equalled nor surpassed.

As a native 'Haligonian' and Cunard historian, I am very proud to share the same birthplace with the man whose perseverance and old-fashioned hard work has produced the most enduring and famous ocean-liner firm in maritime history.

May the name 'Cunard' and the instantly recognisable burnt-red and black funnels continue to be seen afloat … making yet more history, for many more years to come.

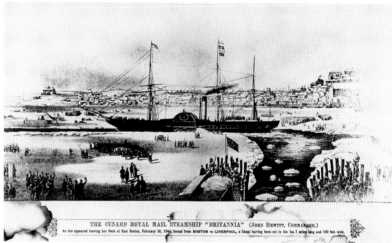

THE CUNARD ROYAL MAIL STEAMSHIP "BRITANNIA" (JOHN HEWITT, COMMANDER.)
As she appeared leaving her Dock at East Boston, February 3d, 1844, bound from BOSTON to LIVERPOOL, a Canal having been cut in the Ice 7 miles long and 100 feet wide.

Above: *Persia* at sea. (R.W. Warwick; *QE2*: The Cunard
Line Flagship Queen Elizabeth II collection)

Above right: The *Britannia* is freed from the ice in Boston
harbour. (Robert Henderson & Doug Cremer collection)

Right: Early Cunard deck scenes give a sense of the
formality aboard. (Robert Henderson & Doug Cremer
collection)

▶ **DID YOU KNOW?**
. . . .

Commodore R.W. Warwick was
instrumental in the creation of a permanent
monument to Sir Samuel Cunard in Halifax,
having suggested the idea after *QM2*'s 2004
maiden visit. It was unveiled by the Halifax
Foundation in 2006.

Oregon was one of the few Cunard steam vessel that did not have an 'ia' name. (R.W. Warwick; *QE2*: The Cunard Line Flagship Queen Elizabeth II collection)

Catalonia was an iron-hulled ship and entered service in 1881. (Robert Henderson & Doug Cremer collection)

3
STAYING ON TOP OF THE COMPETITION

… in every way, excellent.

The single sentence dedicated to steerage in Cunard's 108-page brochure

for Lucania and Campania

In 1884 and 1885 Cunard introduced two new express liners, *Umbria* and *Etruria*. The largest liners then in service, they were able to achieve a top speed of 19.5 knots thanks to their powerful reciprocating engines and single-screw propellers. Both vessels carried auxiliary sails, the last Cunard ships to do so. These ships introduced refrigeration to the transatlantic trade, which removed the need to carry livestock aboard. Not only did *Umbria* and *Etruria* offer passengers a greater choice of meals, but also a vastly improved smell aboard.

Cunard was not to remain at the top of the game for long, however. Inman Line introduced their twin-screw ships, *City of New York* and *City of Paris*, in 1888, while White Star Line had plans for their own twin-screwed ships, with *Teutonic* entering service in 1889 and *Majestic* in 1890. The twin-screw ships were both faster and more reliable than the Cunard duo and Cunard's express service soon required updating again to get back to the peak position. That was to happen with Cunard's first twin-screw vessels, *Lucania* and *Campania*, which were launched in 1893.

Campania and *Lucania* were built by the Fairfield Shipbuilding and Engineering Company, Scotland. At the time, this yard was one of the biggest suppliers of Royal Navy warships. As with many of the Cunard ships that came before them, *Campania* and *Lucania* were built to government specification, with some of the funding for their building being provided by the British Government.

Both ships were designed for speed, with enormous triple-expansion engines that spanned three decks. Their giant engines produced 31,000hp, which gave them a service speed of 22 knots and allowed them to complete a transatlantic crossing in under six days. *Campania* entered service in April 1893 and captured the Atlantic speed record from Inman's *City of Paris* on her second crossing. *Lucania* took the record from her sister ship the following year, holding the record until 1898.

In addition to being the fastest ships on the Atlantic, *Campania* and *Lucania* were also the largest, most luxurious and some of the safest vessels at sea. Each ship was an impressive 12,950 tons, with furnishings

> '
> **Broadcaster Anthony Davis has always had a love of ocean liners and is a regular aboard the Cunard fleet:**
>
> For me, Cunard is about transatlantic crossings, reliving the golden age and reminding ourselves what life was like before jet air travel; before time was of the essence.
>
> I first travelled on *QE2* in 1975, cruising from Southampton to Tenerife and Madeira. I was just six months old and was the youngest passenger on board. When I boarded for the second time, in 1983, for a transatlantic two-way crossing, I could remember where everything was. It was like an out-of-body experience. We got caught up in the infamous storm of '83, off the Bay of Biscay. At the age of nine, I was excited by the vast swells, waves and smashing windows of the Double Down Room.
>
> Nearly twenty years later, I travelled on all three maiden transatlantic crossings on board *QM2*, *Queen Victoria* and *Queen Elizabeth*. Whilst the handcrafted woods have been replaced with synthetic anti-flammable materials, and the clientele may lack the etiquette and class of yesteryear, there is still something magical about a long, slow ocean crossing where you can feel completely alone, amongst your thoughts, without the distraction of Wi-Fi – and have enough time to consume six delicious meals a day.
> '

that included Persian carpets and velvet drapes. Their first-class drawing rooms were 60ft by 30ft and their first-class dining room could seat 430 guests in style.

To ensure the reliability of these ships the engines were located in separate, watertight compartments. This allowed Cunard to do away with auxiliary sails; the masts, which were no longer required, were instead converted to flagpoles. As well as the watertight compartments for the engines, the ships each had sixteen transverse watertight compartments, with each ship able to stay afloat in the event of any two compartments being flooded.

These safety measures were important in case the ships were ever called up for military service. In the event of damage or flooding to one engine, the other would be able to remain in service, hopefully allowing the ship to continue to make way under her own steam.

In 1901, *Lucania*, *Campania*, *Umbria* and *Etruria* were fitted with Marconi wireless technology. It was now possible to send messages to other ships and to shoreside when in range. This was a huge step forward in terms of safety, but it also introduced new entertainments for the passengers aboard. Cunard ships introduced the *Cunard Daily Bulletin*, a daily newspaper for those aboard that outlined communications between the ship and other wireless stations. This helped to reduce the feeling of isolation for those aboard and also provided some amusement.

Etruria made use of her auxiliary sails in 1902 when her propeller shaft developed cracks whilst at sea. She was rigged and sailed to a nearby ship that towed her to the Azores for repairs.

Umbria had her own moment of drama in 1903, when a tip-off led the police to discover an explosive waiting to be loaded on to the ship. The bomb was defused and the ship made way without any damage.

Etruria and her sister *Umbria* had a single-screw propeller and auxiliary sails. (Michael Pocock/Maritime Quest)

The *Umbria* underway. (Robert Henderson & Doug Cremer collection)

All Cunarders carried a cat to look after any rats. (Robert Henderson & Doug Cremer collection)

Lucania was a new breed of Cunarder, running on twin screws. (Ian Boyle/Simplon Postcards)

Lucania and her sister *Campania* didn't require sails and had oversized funnels. (Ian Boyle/Simplon Postcards)

This artist's impression of *Campania* shows her looking far larger than the sailing ships and tugs. (Ian Boyle/Simplon Postcards)

Campania was long and sleek with two giant funnels. (Ian Boyle/Simplon Postcards)

Campania underway offers an impressive profile. (Ian Boyle/Simplon Postcards)

▶ DID YOU KNOW?

Marconi wireless was invented in 1894 by 20-year-old Italian scientist Guglielmo Marconi.

Above: The funnels of *Campania* (pictured) and *Lucania* were the largest in the world. (Michael Pocock/ Maritime Quest)

Left: *Campania*, as depicted in a period postcard. (Ian Boyle/Simplon Postcards)

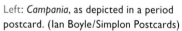

Left: *Saxonia*'s single funnel and four masts were common traits on liners of her era. (Ian Boyle/ Simplon Postcards)

► **DID YOU KNOW?** . . . . . .

Lucania caught fire while in Liverpool in 1909. Despite initial plans to refurbish her, it was decided the damage was too great and the ship was scrapped.

Saxonia in a period postcard symbolising 'hands across the sea' between the United States and Britain. (Ian Boyle/Simplon Postcards)

This artist's impression sought to emphasise *Saxonia*'s bulk. (Ian Boyle/Simplon Postcards)

Above left: An artist's impression of *Saxonia* at sea. (Ian Boyle/Simplon Postcards)

Above: *Albania* (7,640 tons) made her maiden voyage on 17 September 1901. (Ian Boyle/Simplon Postcards)

Left: Dining aboard *Umbria* wasn't as luxurious as we experience today. (Robert Henderson & Doug Cremer collection)

4

GETTING THERE FASTER

I have come to the conclusion that gearing between engines and screw shafting will be essential.

Charles Parsons

With so many competitors all challenging for supremacy on the North Atlantic Ocean it was inevitable that Cunard ships would be overtaken in size, speed and luxury. In the final years of the nineteenth century and early years of the twentieth century a number of ships were launched by Cunard's German rivals that took the records from the Cunard liners.

Kaiser Wilhem der Grosse was launched by Norddeutscher Lloyd in 1897. The following year, she became the first German liner to take the westbound speed record. At 655ft long and more than 14,000 gross tons, she easily outstripped Cunard's express liners *Campania* and *Lucania*.

She was in turn outdone by Hamburg-Amerika's *Deutschland*, which entered service in 1900 and proved faster and more luxurious than her rival. At 16,502 tons and 680ft in length, she was also larger. Norddeutscher Lloyd responded by introducing *Kaiser Wilhelm II*, which commenced her maiden voyage on 14 April 1903. Bigger still than the *Deutschland*, she was 706ft long and 25,530 gross tons.

The size and scope of the German liners was not the only concern for Cunard. The White Star Line had commenced a building programme of their own, which introduced their 'Big Four' into service. The ships, *Celtic, Cedric, Baltic* and *Adriatic*, were all over 700ft in length and their tonnage eclipsed Brunel's infamous white elephant, the *Great Eastern*, for the first time.

This left Cunard in a quandary. The line was not in a strong financial position at the time, though they had managed to resist an attempt to purchase the line by American financier J.P. Morgan in the early twentieth century. Morgan had acquired a number of Cunard's rivals, including White Star Line and the American Line (which had absorbed the Inman Line in 1893), and these companies, along with many others, were re-organised into the International Mercantile Marine Co. (IMM Co.). To make matters worse, IMM Co. had created an alliance with the German lines, adding further pressure to Cunard's bottom line.

As a result, Cunard could not simply build new liners to eclipse the German or White Star ships. Instead they laid down plans for two smaller vessels, which would prove the efficiency of the turbine technology at powering their ships over the more traditional reciprocating engines.

Carmania and *Caronia* were built at the John Brown Shipyard in Clydebank. They were near identical and ushered in a number of new design features in addition to their competing propulsion systems. Both ships were built with high sides and their funnels were painted in different proportion to previous vessels.

Caronia was fitted with reciprocating engines. Though these were the most powerful of their type – eight-cylinder quadruple-expansion engines – she was not able to match the speed or efficiency of *Carmania*. *Carmania* had been fitted with the Parsons Turbine and was the first of the Cunard vessels to use this technology.

The Parsons Turbine was invented in 1884 by Charles Parsons. He had proved the ability of the turbine to propel a vessel by fitting it to a boat named *Turbinia*, and sailing it through Queen Victoria's naval review in 1897. *Turbinia* easily eclipsed the speed of the naval vessels. Parsons' cheeky gamble paid off, with the navy entering discussions with him and soon afterwards beginning to power their new-build ships with this technology.

Merchant shipping was a little slower to catch on. Though aware of the possibilities the new technology provided, it was a great investment for the shipping companies to retrain their engineers to ensure optimum operation of the turbines. Thus, Cunard built two almost identical vessels to test if the efficiencies of the turbine would in fact be worth the investment.

Carmania proved that turbines were more economical than reciprocating engines. (Ian Boyle/Simplon Postcards)

▶ **DID YOU KNOW?** . . . .

Lusitania and *Mauretania*'s names are longer when compared to earlier liners. This was done as Cunard felt their size and scale deserved an extra syllable.

It didn't take long for *Carmania* to prove the case. Having entered service in 1905, on the Liverpool to New York route, *Carmania* quickly showed that she was able to achieve greater speeds with less fuel. Though she was not a record-breaker she had proved an important point to Cunard. As a result, Cunard adopted the turbine technology for their subsequent new builds.

But, in order to become truly competitive on the North Atlantic again, Cunard knew they needed to build new express liners that could recapture the speed record and the attention of the public. The British Admiralty was to assist in this matter.

With Cunard being the last of the large British-owned transatlantic shipping companies, the Admiralty was keen to ensure that they remained competitive and viable, as well as ensuring that a British line was able to challenge for the Atlantic speed record. As a result, they agreed to give Cunard financial assistance to allow them to build what would become known as their 'Ocean Greyhounds'. The conditions of the financial assistance were that the two ships would be very fast – able to achieve speeds of 24 knots – and that they would be able to be converted into armed merchant cruisers if ever the need arose.

WHITE STAR LINE.

TWIN-SCREW R.M.S. "CELTIC." 21,026 TONS.

White Star Line's *Celtic* was the largest liner in the world, causing problems for Cunard. (Ian Boyle/ Simplon Postcards)

With a loan of £2,600,000, Cunard laid down two new vessels: the *Mauretania* at Swan Hunter & Wigham Richardson in Newcastle and the *Lusitania* at the John Brown shipyard in Clydebank. Both yards were given the same general schematic but were encouraged to compete with each other to build the better ship.

The result was two ships that were vastly different in some ways, yet very similar in others. In external appearance the two ships had very similar hulls, with the main difference being in the location and design of their on-deck air vents and their bridges. *Mauretania* sported large scoop style vents, whereas *Lusitania* was completed with much more streamlined vents. *Mauretania*'s bridge was set higher on the ship, while *Lusitania*'s was set a deck lower, adding to her streamlined appearance.

Both ships were fitted with turbines as their propulsion system; however, when *Lusitania* – which was completed first – began sea trials it was discovered that the turbines caused significant vibrations at high speeds. *Lusitania* was returned to the shipyard and fitted with additional strengthening beams and *Mauretania* was also completed with the same design. In addition, the propellers were redesigned in an effort to reduce vibrations.

Norddeutscher Lloyd,
Bremen.

Left: *Kaiser Wilhelm der Grosse* was the first of the four-funnel liners and eclipsed Cunard's speed. (Ian Boyle/Simplon Postcards)

Below left: The accommodation aboard *Caronia* and *Carmania* was very pleasant. (Robert Henderson & Doug Cremer Collection)

Below: The steam turbine was a revolution in engineering, saving fuel, time and maintenance. (Robert Henderson & Doug Cremer Collection)

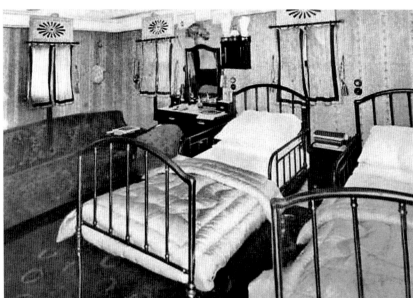

Gaynor van Deventer has worked aboard the Cunard fleet for many years in the ship's ocean bookshops:

Growing up partly in Durban, I can recall seeing the Union Castle ships sailing in and out of the harbour as well as *QE2* in Cape Town on 10 November 1970. It was a huge thing for our family to see this vessel – as she was famous, even in South Africa – though we knew we would never be able to afford to travel on her. I then dreamt of one day being able to sail on a ship, never thinking that it would be as a crew member. A few decades later, I was fortunate to secure a position on *QM2*. It was absolutely mind-blowing to step on board the vessel for the very first time; I was dumbfounded by the elegance and stature she presented. I enjoyed working on *QM2* for two and a half years. During this time I met a few celebrities. I was on board *QM2* and witnessed the meeting up with *Queen Mary* in Long beach California – what a memorable occasion that was.

I changed position and changed ship. The *QE2* was to be my home for the last two years of her career. This was a dream of four decades that finally came true; I was not just looking and admiring this magnificent vessel from a distance, but actually boarding her in Fort Lauderdale as a crew member. I could only understand what I had been hearing about the *QE2* once I set foot on her myself; she had a totally different feel, homely warmth, even though she was older and her interior was not as modern as the *QM2*. She still had her own classic grandeur. In a way it was like stepping into a movie. I was on board when she did her final world voyage in 2008, and I also was present when HM Queen Elizabeth came to say her last goodbye in June 2008. I left *QE2* in July 2008 to join her new sister, *Queen Victoria*. I had the honour of working with Captain Ian McNaught and there I got to meet many of our repeat guests, and currently still get to see some of these guests who are now sailing on the current Queens.

I must confess, it was very different to come to a brand new ship again. I was glad that I did not do the final trip on *QE2*, as even in the short while that I was working on her, I grew to love her and it saddened me to know that we are not going to have her in the fleet for too much longer. I saw heart-wrenching moments when guests said their last goodbyes, even if it was six months before she was retiring. The final voyage sold out in record time. I have since mainly been sailing on *Queen Victoria*; I have had a very short while on *Queen Elizabeth*, and have been back on *QM2* for the odd cover, but do enjoy *Queen Victoria* at the moment. I have had the honour of working with Commodore Ron Warwick on *QM2* and I have also been on board for many of the special occasions when the three Queens have met up and on 5 June 2012, during the Diamond Jubilee celebrations, I was on *Queen Victoria*. I had a brief stay on *Queen Elizabeth* and it was a bit like déjà vu, so familiar yet so different from *Queen Victoria* was she.

I am very grateful that I got a chance to experience what I once could only dream of. Cunard Line is unique in the sense that even though we are present day, we do still enjoy the pleasures of traditional British lifestyle, afternoon teas, formal evenings, baked Alaska. When the guests are all dressed in true formal attire, it is so beautiful and almost takes one back in time again.

Internally the ships were very different. *Lusitania*'s interior was light and bright, making extensive use of plasterwork. The first-class accommodation was completed largely in a Louis XVI style, while second-class mirrored first-class, albeit on a smaller scale.

Mauretania was completed in a quintessential Edwardian style and extensive dark wood panelling throughout. The ship used electric lighting to illuminate public rooms, while the first-class dining room was completed in a Francis I style.

Both ships were able to meet their speed targets, with *Lusitania* first, and then *Mauretania* winning the Blue Riband for their crossings. *Mauretania* went on to hold the speed record from 1909 to 1929 with a time of four days, ten hours and fifty-one minutes.

The two ships proved very popular with the travelling public and were able to recapture Cunard's place in the market. They were not to remain the most luxurious liners on the North Atlantic for long, however. In 1910, White Star launched the first of the Olympic-class liners. *Olympic* and her sister ship, *Titanic*, ushered in many new luxuries including a Turkish bath, squash court and opulent parlour suites complete with private balconies.

Despite their speed, *Lusitania* and *Mauretania* were unable to complete a weekly transatlantic schedule; thus, Cunard required a third ship for their express service. Rather than build another ship along the same lines as their 'Ocean Greyhounds', they instead opted to build a slightly larger and more luxurious (albeit slower) ship to compete directly with White Star in terms of luxury.

Aquitania was laid down at the John Brown Shipyard in December 1910. Before she was completed, the sinking of White Star Line's *Titanic* on her maiden voyage shocked the world, leaving lasting changes to the shipping industry. Having struck an iceberg on 14 April 1912 at 11.40 p.m., *Titanic* sank early the next morning with a considerable loss of life.

Cunard's liner *Carpathia* rescued all 705 survivors of the *Titanic* disaster. An intermediate liner that had been built in 1903, *Carpathia* was renowned for her excellent accommodation, the ship's interiors being superior to many other liners.

Immediately following the loss of *Titanic*, two inquiries were set up to attribute blame for the disaster, as well as recommend solutions to ensure such a tragedy never occurred again. The first inquiry was held in the United States while the second was held in Great Britain.

Many of those lost aboard *Titanic* died because the ship, like most ships at the time, did not carry enough lifeboats for all the people on board. Lifeboat carriage aboard ships registered in Great Britain was regulated by the British Board of Trade, which hadn't updated the provision of lifeboat seats since ships were far smaller than *Titanic*. Furthermore, the regulations specified lifeboat carriage based on the vessel's tonnage, rather than its passenger capacity. Calls were immediately made for this archaic practice to be fixed, resulting in lifeboat space for every person aboard. The inquiries further resulted in a long overdue review of safety regulations as well as the establishment of the Safety of Life at Sea (SOLAS) provisions and a marine survey with the task of identifying icebergs.

Shipbuilders also made changes to designs, which were incorporated into *Aquitania*. This new Cunarder was larger than her fleet mates, at

The *Carmania* was built as a test case for the turbine engine. (Ian Boyle/Simplon Postcards)

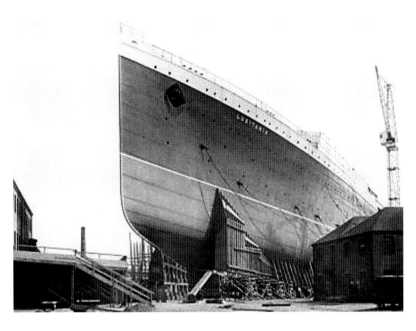

Lusitania's sleek bow awaiting launch. (Robert Henderson & Doug Cremer Collection)

Lusitania leaving the Clyde after completion. (Robert Henderson & Doug Cremer Collection)

45,647 tons and 901ft long, and was designed to take the travelling public by storm. Her graceful exterior and elegant interiors earned her the nickname 'Ship Beautiful', allowing Cunard to directly compete against the elegant White Star liners.

With safety changes incorporated, *Aquitania* was a far safer ship than those that had come before her. Cunard advertised her safety features, making particular mention of her lifeboat capacity, with seats for all aboard. While pre-*Titanic* ships were often designed to minimise the visual impact of lifeboats, *Aquitania*'s were visible on the deck of the ship, ensuring there were no misconceptions with the general public. The company also emphasised the inclusion of extra watertight compartments that allowed the ship to float with five compartments flooded, either foreword or aft.

Like her running mates, *Aquitania* was completed under the auxiliary armed cruisers agreement, meaning she was available to be called into military service in the event of war, an event that would prove all too soon in arriving.

Lusitania's propellers were each powered by a separate turbine. (Robert Henderson & Doug Cremer Collection)

Towering over the wharf, *Lusitania* looks enormous in this image. (Robert Henderson & Doug Cremer Collection)

Lusitania at New York in 1907. (Michael Pocock/Maritime Quest)

Mauretania entered service several months after *Lusitania*. (Ian Boyle/Simplon Postcards)

Q. T. S. S., Mauretania, (THE LARGEST VESSEL IN THE WORLD,) LEAVING THE TYNE.

S.S. MAURETANIA

Above: *Mauretania* makes for an impressive sight when at sea. (Michael Pocock/Maritime Quest)

Mauretania was built at Swan Hunter, Newcastle upon Tyne. (Ian Boyle/Simplon Postcards)

Liner leaving Landing Stage, Liverpool

▶ DID YOU KNOW?

Aquitania was one deck taller, 114ft longer and 10ft wider than *Lusitania*.

Mauretania in Liverpool. (Ian Boyle/Simplon Postcards)

Mauretania at Fishguard. (Ian Boyle/Simplon Postcards)

Mauretania at anchor, taking on passengers and supplies. (Ian Boyle/Simplon Postcards)

An artist's impression of *Mauretania* near smaller sailing ships. (Ian Boyle/Simplon Postcards)

This postcard of *Mauretania* was designed to showcase her speed and size. (Ian Boyle/ Simplon Postcards)

FASTEST STEAMERS IN THE WORLD.

CUNARD LINE

Mauretania was the world's fastest liner until 1929. (Ian Boyle/Simplon Postcards)

Lusitania, at the time one of the world's largest and fastest liners. (Robert Henderson & Doug Cremer Collection)

CUNARD LINE

S.S. MAURETANIA entering New York Harbour.

A Cunard postcard of the new Mauretania; note the inaccuracy of the bridge design in this artist's impression. (Ian Boyle/Simplon Postcards)

Lusitania towers over the awaiting vehicles in New York. (Robert Henderson & Doug Cremer Collection)

Lusitania sailing fast, thanks to her turbines. (Robert Henderson & Doug Cremer Collection)

There was a lift for first-class passengers aboard *Lusitania* and *Mauretania*. (Robert Henderson & Doug Cremer Collection)

Lusitania's first-class dining room, complete with ornate dome. (Robert Henderson & Doug Cremer Collection)

The veranda café aboard *Mauretania*. (Robert Henderson & Doug Cremer Collection)

The boat deck of the *Mauretania*, where passengers came to promenade. (Robert Henderson & Doug Cremer Collection)

The first-class dining room aboard *Mauretania*. (Robert Henderson & Doug Cremer Collection)

5

THE FIRST WORLD WAR

We have made a request to the German Government that we shall have a satisfactory assurance as to the Belgium neutrality before midnight tonight. The German reply to our request was unsatisfactory.

British Prime Minister Herbert Henry Asquith, Earl of Oxford
on Britain's declaration of war against Germany

Cunard's new liner, *Aquitania*, entered service for Cunard on 30 May 1914, one day after the Canadian Pacific Steamships vessel *Empress of Ireland* sank with the loss of 1,012 lives. The disaster marred the festivities planned for *Aquitania*'s maiden voyage with many passengers on board feeling a strong sense of unease during the journey.

In the past decade, Cunard's services had expanded considerably. Not only had the line introduced three express liners, their intermediate services had increased significantly. The line had also increased its ability to carry cargo. This expansion was bolstered by the 1911 purchase of the Thompson Line. The acquisition included the *Albania*, *Ascania* and *Ausonia*. This tonnage was supplemented by the acquisition of the Anchor Line that same year, which added valuable tonnage and routes to the business with the aim of creating a profitable peacetime enterprise.

However, plans for a profitable peacetime service came to a halt less than two months after the *Aquitania*'s maiden voyage. With Britain, France, Russia and their allies at war with Germany and her allies, the First World War had commenced, and Cunard would face its greatest challenge yet as many of their ships were requisitioned for government service.

Having been built under the auxiliary armed merchant cruisers agreement, *Aquitania* and *Mauretania* were both taken up from service and given refits to make them into armed merchant cruisers. A number of Cunard's earlier express liners, along with their intermediate liners were also called into government service.

Lusitania, though built under the auxiliary armed merchant cruiser agreement, and designed for conversion, never entered into government service. Instead she was kept in merchant service, operating a reduced schedule across the North Atlantic. *Mauretania*, with its almost identical design, did not remain an armed merchant cruiser for long. Her design, though fast, proved unsuitable for the purpose and she was returned to Cunard. The reduced demand for passenger crossings, however, saw her laid up rather than re-entered into service.

The heroic *Carpathia* was sunk during the First World War. (Michael Pocock/Maritime Quest)

The war soon spread to the ocean and the North Atlantic became a dangerous place for ships to transit. In an attempt to combat this danger, *Lusitania*'s funnels were painted black in an attempt to disguise her and she sailed for a time under the then neutral United States flag, though once US President Wilson wrote a letter of protest to the British Admiralty, this practice was stopped. From then on *Lusitania* sailed with no flag at all.

On 7 May 1915, a torpedo fired by German submarine U-20 struck *Lusitania*. Two explosions ensued and the ship sank off the coast of Ireland with a loss of 1,198 lives. The tragic incident is said to have been a contributing factor in the United States entering into the conflict on the side of the Allies, as there had been American citizens on board who were killed when the ship sank.

After the sinking of the *Lusitania* there was no Cunard ship left in merchant service on the England to New York route. *Mauretania* was intended to be brought back into service but, before this happened, the ship was once again requisitioned by the Admiralty, this time as a troopship, carrying soldiers to the Dardanelles.

In August 1915, *Mauretania* was converted to a hospital ship and placed into service evacuating the wounded from Gallipoli. The ship's interiors were reconfigured once again, this time using the space throughout for hospital beds, wards and operating theatres. The hull was painted white and a series of large red crosses were emblazoned along the vessel to identify her as a hospital ship.

Aquitania made three voyages as a troopship, before she too was converted to a hospital ship. The transition to hospital duties was made possible by the United States' entry into the war. At the time the United States entered the conflict on the side of the Allies, the majority

Aquitania's magnificent Palladian Room. (Robert Henderson & Doug Cremer collection)

Aquitania is launched at John Brown in Clydebank. (Ian Boyle/Simplon Postcards)

Aquitania, Cunard's largest ship, takes to the water. (Ian Boyle/Simplon Postcards)

of the large German liners were docked in American ports. American authorities seized these ships, including the Vaterland and Imperator, and placed them into service as troop carriers for America.

Many of Cunard's intermediate liners had also been taken up from trade. This included Laconia and Franconia, which had entered service in 1912 and 1911 respectively, as well as Carpathia, the ship that had rescued the survivors of the Titanic disaster. None of these ships would survive the war.

Cunard's 18,150-ton Franconia was lost in October 1916, when she was torpedoed off the coast of Malta by UB-47. The subsequent sinking resulted in the loss of twelve men, with the survivors collected by Dover Castle.

Franconia's sister ship, Laconia, was also lost during the war. Laconia was operating as an armed merchant cruiser when she was torpedoed by U-50 off the English coast; again, twelve people died.

Carpathia was lost during 1918 while steaming in a convoy off the coast of England. Three German torpedoes sealed the ship's fate. Five crewmembers were lost, with the survivors being collected by HMS Snowdrop.

That same year after being recommissioned as a troop carrier, Aquitania collided with the USS Shaw, which was assigned to escort the large Cunard liner. The Shaw's helm had jammed, causing the ship to lose manoeuvrability and leaving the stricken vessel in Aquitania's path. With the captain aware that depth charges were stored in the aft end of the Shaw, he quickly placed the vessel full astern resulting in Aquitania hitting the ship amidships, and though Shaw was sliced in two, the captain's actions had averted a greater disaster.

▶ DID YOU KNOW? . . . .

Campania and Lucania's reciprocating engines were so large that they protruded above the ships' hulls. To protect them, designers created a deck house over the engines.

R. M. S. Aquitania (Cunard Line).
Length 902 ft. Breadth 97 ft.
Depth 92 ft. 6 inches.
Tonnage 47,000. Speed 23 knots.

Left: A postcard of Cunard's *Aquitania*; which inaccurately depicts *Mauretania*. (Ian Boyle/Simplon Postcards)

Below left: Warships and merchant ships alike became targets during the war. (George Frame collection)

Below: The waters around Great Britain became a war zone at the outbreak of the First World War. (George Frame collection)

'Elaine MacKay is a name many Cunard cruisers will know; she worked with the line for twenty-three years:

Little did I know, when I went on board *Cunard Princess* in 1980 to do arts and crafts for a one-week cruise, that in less than two years I would give up my teaching career and launch a love affair with an ocean liner that would last just over twenty-three years (but still lingers on today). That one-week cruise hooked me on the joy of cruising. After several such cruises the cruise director, John Butt, said he had recommended me for the *QE2* world cruise as Spanish linguist. I never did that job but joined *QE2* in New York on Columbus Day 1982 as programmer and then social directress, and made more discoveries than Christopher ever thought of. It was the hardest working, most enjoyable job I ever had. I loved the history of Cunard Line and enjoyed sharing it with passengers each voyage. What a majestic lineage for the Great Lady. The ship's beauty, her majestic glide (and sometimes chopping twists in gale-force winds) just added to the thrill. I just loved the transatlantics; after all, that was her heritage and what the Clydebank shipyards built her for and we never knew what Mother Nature would throw our way.

But my favourite part of being on *QE2* was the passengers, celebrity entertainers and crew I met over the years; it truly was a family atmosphere. They all shared in the joy that *QE2* brought. Many pax [passengers] said coming on board was like coming home, and coming back from leave felt like coming home to me. While a big ship for her time, she had a warm, homely atmosphere. I don't really think any other ship has ever had the special connection with the passengers and crew that *QE2* did. World cruise embarkation day was certainly old home week. On any regular embarkation I would always greet our regular return passengers but on a world cruise there were so many more welcome-back greetings and, of course, what other ship could ever dare hang out a 'Welcome Home' banner for returning passengers? They really loved that. I am still in touch with many 'old' passengers and they tell me they have gone on other ships, and they were nice, *but*, they were not the *QE2*.

I remember the 'train parties' in the earlier days, such fun; the Country Fayre; a singer (whom I will not name) mooning the poor guys driving the mules through the Panama Canal; a pax asking Dr Norman Vincent Peale during an interview with me if 'His power of positive thinking had a positive effect on his sex life in later life' – you could have heard a pin drop. I have so many stories and happy memories. I miss my time on board *QE2* but it is such a joy to still be in touch with so many old my shipboard friends. '

Cunard's old express liner *Campania*, which had been laid up awaiting scrap prior to the war, was sold to the British Government. She was converted to an aircraft carrier and later earned the distinction of being the first ship to launch aircraft whilst underway.

Caronia, *Carmania* and *Saxonia* were all requisitioned for war service and each of the ships survived; however, tonnage from the Cunard-owned subsidiaries was not so fortunate. The company lost a number of ships from their Anchor Line venture, along with all three ships they had been awarded from the Uranium SS Co. as war reparations in 1916.

► **DID YOU KNOW?**

In 1916, Cunard's Anchor Line purchased a controlling share in the Donaldson Line, forming Anchor-Donaldson Line.

OCEAN STEAMSHIPS.

CUNARD

EUROPE VIA LIVERPOOL
LUSITANIA

Fastest and Largest Steamer
now in Atlantic Service Sails
SATURDAY, MAY 1, 10 A.M.
Transylvania, Fri., May 7, 5 P.M.
Orduna, - - Tues., May 18, 10 A.M.
Tuscania, - - Fri., May 21, 5 P.M.
LUSITANIA, Sat., May 29, 10 A.M.
Transylvania, Fri., June 4, 5 P.M.
Gibraltar—Genoa—Naples—Piraeus
S.S. Carpathia, Thur., May 13, Noon

NOTICE!

TRAVELLERS intending to embark on the Atlantic voyage are reminded that a state of war exists between Germany and her allies and Great Britain and her allies; that the zone of war includes the waters adjacent to the British Isles; that, in accordance with formal notice given by the Imperial German Government, vessels flying the flag of Great Britain, or of any of her allies, are liable to destruction in those waters and that travellers sailing in the war zone on ships of Great Britain or her allies do so at their own risk.

IMPERIAL GERMAN EMBASSY
WASHINGTON, D. C., APRIL 22, 1915.

Lusitania's sailing schedule above the infamous notice from the Imperial German Embassy. (Michael Pocock/Maritime Quest)

The year 2015 will see the centenary of *Lusitania's* sinking. (Robert Henderson & Doug Cremer collection)

Cunard's *Aquitania* served as a hospital ship during the First World War. (Ian Boyle/ Simplon Postcards)

Imperator (later renamed *Berengaria*) was Cunard's compensation for the loss of *Lusitania*. (Robert Henderson & Doug Cremer collection)

6

THE INTERWAR YEARS

Launched the new *Queen Mary* today; pity it rained.

HM Queen Mary *journal entry following the*
launch of Cunard-White Star's flagship, RMS Queen Mary

Following the cessation of hostilities, a number of the Cunard ships remained in government service. *Aquitania*, *Mauretania*, *Caronia*, *Carmania* and *Saxonia* were all used in the repatriation of American and Canadian troops.

Aquitania and *Mauretania* were able to re-enter passenger service by the end of 1919, after being returned to Cunard and extensively refitted. Without the *Lusitania*, however, Cunard could not complete their three-ship express service. They resolved this issue when the British Government were awarded a number of German liners as war reparations.

The Hamburg-Amerika liners *Imperator* and *Bismarck* were two of the largest ships of their day. Cunard and White Star Line jointly purchased these ships from the British Government.

Cunard operated *Imperator*, which was one of the more luxurious ships on the market at 900ft long and 52,200 tons. White Star Line was to operate *Bismarck*, which was still under construction at the time

of purchase. The third of the large Hamburg-Amerika ships, *Vaterland*, was retained by the United States, becoming the United States Line's flagship *Leviathan*.

Cunard gave *Imperator* a refurbishment and entered her into service as their third express liner in March 1920. She did not remain in service under that name for long, however, and was soon given a major overhaul and renamed as *Berengaria*, becoming the flagship of the Cunard fleet.

With *Berengaria* in service, Cunard were able to re-establish their express services relatively quickly, which meant that they were at the head of the competition again. The German lines had had to surrender their ships to the Allies and were therefore no longer a threat. The IMM Co. had dissolved prior to the war and, as a result, the individual companies no longer had the strength to take on the Cunard Line.

Even White Star Line, now a British-flagged line again, was not able to effectively compete with Cunard's express service. Their own three-ship express service was in tatters. They had lost *Titanic* to an iceberg prior to

FASTEST OCEAN SERVICE
IN THE WORLD

CUNARD

SOUTHAMPTON, CHERBOURG
AND NEW YORK

R.M.S. "MAURETANIA"   R.M.S. "BERENGARIA"   R.M.S. "AQUITANIA"

Above: Cunard's premier liners, *Mauretania*, *Berengaria* and *Aquitania*. (Ian Boyle/Simplon Postcards)

the war and *Britannic* to a mine during the war. As a result the line only had *Olympic* in service. *Bismarck* took time to complete; however, when she was launched as *Majestic* for White Star Line she was one of the greatest ships in service. At 955ft and 56,551 tons, she outstripped even the *Berengaria* and held the title of world's largest ship.

White Star Line also purchased the incomplete Norddeutscher Lloyd liner *Columbus* from His Majesty's Shipping Controller. Renamed *Homeric*, the ship was smaller and slower than their other express liners and was still a coal-burning ship, making it more time-consuming to refuel between voyages.

In 1922, the *Tyrrhenia* entered service for the Cunard-owned Anchor Line. Built by William Beardmore and Co., the 16,200-ton vessel operated for a short period for Anchor Line before she was refurbished in 1924 with cruising in mind and renamed *Lancastria*. From here on she sailed under the Cunard flag.

Cunard began to build new ships, including their A-class liners, so called because their names all started with the letter A. The fleet consisted of *Antonia*, *Andania*, *Ausonia*, *Aurania*, *Alaunia* and *Ascania*. The first three of the fleet were commissioned in 1922, with *Aurania* in 1924 and the final two in 1925.

With these intermediate liners, Cunard operated services between Europe and North America and Canada. These routes proved very profitable and increased the awareness of Cunard around the world.

The former *Imperator* was refurbished and renamed *Berengaria*. (Ian Boyle/Simplon Postcards)

Berengaria was a welcome addition to the Cunard fleet. (Ian Boyle/Simplon Postcards)

> Jamie Firth served on several of the Cunard *Queens* and recalls his affections for the Cunard Line:
>
> It is a privilege to have a career with Cunard, continuing the legacy that has passed into our care to hand to yet another generation. I have worked with many nationalities, whom over time have become more family than just work colleagues. This has given it a feeling of returning home rather than a workplace each contract. I feel so lucky to have a job that I fully enjoy and that has given me and my family the chance to experience so many countries, meeting so many wonderful passengers along the way.

Aquitania's design was so exquisite, inside and out, that she was nicknamed the Ship Beautiful throughout her career. (Ian Boyle/Simplon Postcards)

Adding to this, Cunard sent its ship, the second *Laconia*, on a world cruise in 1923. This was to become a Cunard tradition, expanding the Cunard offering and really entering them into the cruising market. Built at Swan Hunter, Newcastle upon Tyne, the *Laconia* was a 19,600-ton vessel. At 601ft long, the ship was of good dimensions to offer a world voyage, providing enough space aboard for the passengers to entertain themselves during the long voyage. She was joined by *Franconia*, which, adding to *Scythia* and *Samaria*, completed the series of four intermediate liners designed to undertake cruises.

Cunard further added to its fleet when it commissioned *Carinthia*, which entered service in 1925. At just over 20,000 tons, she was a relatively small ship; however, she was notable for being designed with winter cruising in mind.

The German lines were not to remain crushed for long. By the time of the stock market crash in 1929, Norddeutscher Lloyd had introduced their new express liners the *Bremen* and the *Europa*. *Bremen* and *Europa* eclipsed the Cunard express liners in size, speed and luxury and their profile radically changed the face of ocean liner design. Their modern hull with cruiser stern was paired with a streamlined superstructure and squat funnels, which gave the ships a contemporary appearance.

The newly formed Italia Line (created when Mussolini nationalised Italy's shipping industry) introduced two new liners and entered the transatlantic race. Placing *Rex* and the *Conte di Savoir* into service in 1932, the line was well placed to offer real competition to the British and German lines. While *Rex* was extremely fast and captured the transatlantic speed record, *Conte di Savoir* is renowned as being the first large liner to feature stabilisation technology.

Cunard responded to these threats by laying down a new ship on 1 December 1930 at John Brown Shipyard. To be an 80,000-ton liner, Hull 534 was intended to win the hearts of the travelling public with its speed and luxury. Cunard was not the only shipping company laying down new ships, however. On 28 June 1928, the White Star Line laid down a new 1,000ft long liner, to be named *Oceanic*.

The design of the new White Star Line ship called for a traditional exterior, which masked her revolutionary machinery. White Star Line, now owned by the Royal Mail Steam Packet Co., had opted for forty diesel engines with the intention of operating the ship at speeds of over 28 knots. However, the cash-poor line was forced to cancel construction in July 1929. The ship was broken up and priority was given to the building of the smaller *Britannic* as well as a sister ship, *Georgic*.

Aquitania against the New York skyline. (Ian Boyle/Simplon Postcards)

Berengaria became Cunard's flagship. (Ian Boyle/Simplon Postcards)

The French Line laid down their 79,000-ton *Normandie* in January 1931. She was to be a rival for Cunard's new ship and also an extremely luxurious and fast ship. *Normandie*'s design was radically different from previous transatlantic liners, with a hydrodynamic hull and turbo-electric engines.

By the time *Normandie* was laid down, the impact of the Great Depression was causing great problems for Cunard. Their ageing fleet were crossing the Atlantic emptier than usual due to the prevailing financial conditions. Furthermore, those passengers who were travelling opted for the newer, faster and more luxurious liners such as *Bremen* or *Rex*.

Cunard attempted to send some of their older tonnage cruising, having moderate success with 'booze cruises' out of America, which was in the midst of Prohibition at the time. But liners such as *Mauretania*, built in 1907 to strict transatlantic specifications, were generally unsuitable as cruise ships and continued to lose money for Cunard.

In December 1931, construction was halted on Hull 534. The partially constructed ship was to lie on the slipway, slowly rusting for the next two years. In the meantime the shipyard force was laid off and the community of Clydebank suffered greatly from the lack of employment available.

The French Line, by contrast, was able to continue construction of their ship thanks to government support. The French Government felt it was important to show competing powers that France could deliver what was the world's most opulent liner in the midst of a global depression. As such, *Normandie* was launched on 29 October 1932 amid much fanfare.

▶ DID YOU KNOW?

Queen Mary's original design had a stern arrangement similar to *Aquitania*, including a separate second-class deck house. This was changed before the ship was built.

Cunard's new flagship *Berengaria*, the former *Imperator*. (Ian Boyle/Simplon Postcards)

Left: *Berengaria* underway. (Ian Boyle/Simplon Postcards)

Centre: *Berengaria* on a still ocean. (Ian Boyle/Simplon Postcards)

Bottom: *Mauretania* was the fastest liner in the world until 1929.
(Ian Boyle/Simplon Postcards)

Unable to complete their new builds, both Cunard and White Star Line each applied to the British Government for financial assistance. The British Government responded to these requests following the receipt of a report by Clydebank MP David Kirkwood. This report explained that the completion of Hull 534 was in the nation's best interests. The government agreed to provide finance to complete the ship and a running mate, on the proviso that Cunard and White Star Line merged.

Negotiations commenced in 1933 and by 1934 an agreement had been made with Cunard maintaining a controlling interest in the newly formed Cunard-White Star Line. With the merger, twelve White Star Liners, including *Olympic*, *Majestic*, *Homeric*, *Britannic*, *Georgic*, *Laurentic*, *Calgaric*, *Doric*, *Adriatic* and *Albertic* joined the Cunard-White Star fleet. The excess of tonnage meant that Cunard-White Star was forced to retire a number of ships. Most of the vessels that were retired were former White Star Line ships, leaving only *Britannic*, *Georgic* and *Laurentic* by the end of the decade; however, Cunarders including *Mauretania* and *Berengaria* were also scrapped.

The merger of the two lines resulted in funds being provided and construction on Hull 534 recommenced in April 1934. HM Queen Mary christened the ship *Queen Mary* on 26 September 1934 at her launch and the new ship moved to fitting out, being completed with art deco interiors. The interiors were designed to be comfortable, rather than opulent, whilst still delivering luxury. As a result, she had a very different feel to her French rival, *Normandie*, which had been completed in a more grand and overstated manner. This interior design difference gave *Queen Mary* an edge over *Normandie* with many passengers.

Queen Mary set sail on her maiden voyage on 27 May 1936. King George V and Queen Mary toured the ship prior to the voyage; with Queen Mary

Berengaria's first-class ballroom was one of the finest rooms at sea. (Ian Boyle/Simplon Postcards)

Berengaria's first-class smoking room was a sight to behold. (Ian Boyle/Simplon Postcards)

Mauretania was smaller than *Aquitania* and *Berengaria* yet remained popular due to her speed. (Ian Boyle/Simplon Postcards)

DID YOU KNOW?

By the 1990s Cunard managed a number of hotels and resorts including:

The Ritz, London
The Dukes, London
The Stafford, London
Hotel Atop the Bellevue, Philadelphia
Watergate, Washington
Hotel La Toc, St Lucia
Paradise Beach, Barbados

writing in her diary of the occasion, 'toured the new *Queen Mary* today. Not as bad as I expected.'

Though fast, *Queen Mary* was not able to capture the Blue Riband on her maiden voyage, which was by now held by the French Line's *Normandie*. Although *Queen Mary* made excellent time during her crossing, she was delayed by fog, making a record-breaking crossing impossible. In August 1936, *Queen Mary* captured the speed record, holding it for a year before losing it to *Normandie* in 1937. A year later she recaptured the record, this time holding it until 1952, with a time of three days, twenty-one hours and forty-eight minutes.

Construction of a running mate for *Queen Mary* commenced on 4 December 1936. Also laid down at the John Brown Shipyard, she was given the yard number Hull 552.

Cunard-White Star also commissioned a smaller 33,000-ton liner, which was built at the Cammell Laird yard. Laid down on 24 May 1937, she was launched as *Mauretania* on 28 July 1938 with Lady Bates (wife of Cunard-White Star's chairman) officiating at the ceremony.

Hull 552 was launched on 27 September 1938 by HM Queen Elizabeth, who named the ship for herself. Following this, the newly christened *Queen Elizabeth* was moved to the fitting-out basin.

The new *Mauretania*'s maiden transatlantic crossing commenced on 17 June 1939, just months before the start of the Second World War. *Queen Elizabeth*, on the other hand, was still in Clydebank when hostilities broke out.

▶ **DID YOU KNOW?**

Queen Mary suffered from a significant rolling problem in her early career. It was said that the *Queen Mary* could 'roll the milk out of a cup of tea'.

Mauretania in cruising white, so painted to help cool the hull of the un-air conditioned liner. (Bill Miller)

Above: *Mauretania* and *Olympic* laid up, awaiting scrap. (Michael Pocock/Maritime Quest)

An artist's impression of *Queen Mary*, with the size of her funnels exaggerated. (Ian Boyle/Simplon Postcards)

Queen Mary's interior was quite different from previous Cunard ships, sporting art deco finishes. (Ian Boyle/Simplon Postcards)

Queen Mary had a children's room, much to the delight of travelling families. (Ian Boyle/Simplon Postcards)

Queen Mary was the pride of the British Merchant Fleet. (Ian Boyle/ Simplon Postcards)

Captain Ian McNaught was QE2's last master and is well known among Cunard loyalists:

QE2, what can I say? Being with her was like being married, it had its ups and downs, but you knew she was something special and yes, I loved her to bits.

Of course, she was not everybody's cup of tea. When she first came out, she was radically different from the old Queens, 'Ships have been boring too long' was the slogan. She was very much a ship of the Sixties. Her only competition at the time on the Atlantic was the beautiful *France*, but the British had been brave, and you had *Oriana*, *Canberra* and *QE2* – all fantastic demonstrations of British ingenuity and a huge leap forward from those traditional ships built after the war to replace huge losses.

I can remember as a schoolboy watching the launch on the television, and already wanting to go to sea, something I had inherited from my father. I was fascinated by her; here was something modern, something of its time, something different.

I did not join her until 1987, after some sixteen years at sea. It was immediately after the re-engine project, and more controversy, just like in the beginning. This time it wasn't turbine problems; this time it was Grimm Wheels falling off, and the ship not being ready for passengers. I can remember seeing a picture of Captain Portet in one of the newspapers, with a really disparaging article about the ship and thinking, 'have I done the right thing?'

Once I joined, I never had any doubts. Yes, she had problems, but she just enveloped you and drew you in and you became part of something greater than yourself.

Transatlantic crossings were fantastic, this four-day dash across the ocean at 29 knots. It was a voyage with real purpose, no matter what the weather, and the ship just took on this four-day routine to entertain the passengers: captain's receptions, cabin parties, church service on Sunday mornings, black-tie dinners, afternoon tea served by waiters with white gloves, and lectures from some of the biggest names around at the time. The ship did not need the outside world for those four days, it was like magic, and before you knew it, you were berthing in Pier 90, Manhattan.

Totally different was the world cruise. After the Christmas Caribbean cruise, the ship would transform itself into a totally different atmosphere, with passengers on board until the end of April for this leisurely circumnavigation of the world. Everybody knew everybody, passengers would book the same cabin year after year, and the whole ship just relaxed and enjoyed itself. How could you not? As well as all the small places, you had three days in Hong Kong, three days in Sydney, and fantastic tours for passengers: safaris in Kenya, Agra in India, the Great Wall of China, just to name a few.

But it was not all about passengers. The heart and soul of the ship was the ship's company, and it was these 1,020 people who made her what she was; it was them who gave the ship her character. To some passengers I don't think it mattered where the ship was, they had come to enjoy the ship and the crew. We had a very close relationship with our passengers, and I think some of the more modern, larger tonnage must miss out on the contact between passengers and crew. There were still many crew members who, when we took her to Dubai in 2008, had been there since the maiden voyage, virtually forty years' service in one ship. I can remember one restaurant manager who only had three ships in his discharge book, *Queen Mary*, *Queen Elizabeth* and *QE2*. The loyalty to QE2 was enormous, and you cannot buy that, or pretend … it was real and tangible – and it did not matter what your job was in the ship, you were part of something special.

There are many special memories for me. I suppose the first time you take command is a unique day; all of a sudden it is all yours and everybody is looking at you to provide order and direction. This is what you have worked for all your life, to be in command of the most famous ship in the world, and sailing out of Southampton that day, having cleared Nab Tower and set speed for New York, to come down from the bridge into the captain's quarters for your supper just made me feel very humble, but proud, and, to be honest, a little nervous. It was the beginning of a great adventure.

In 2007, we had a cruise around the UK to celebrate her 40th anniversary since launching on the Clyde, and I had the great thrill of taking her to River Tyne, my home port. As we came up from Southampton the weather just got worse and worse, until we arrived off the Tyne in black skies, driving rain and strong winds. 'Sorry we are not going in,' I said. I could see that the locals had turned out in their thousands, and it was a tidal river, so we only had a short window. Well, we went round three times off the entrance until, on the fourth time round, you could see blue sky up river and the evening sun appearing and the wind beginning to drop, so in we went. I shall never forget that welcome, thousands had waited so patiently in the wind and the rain to see her come in, and to be able to bring my ship home made me feel quite humble and proud.

We also had the honour of entertaining HM the Queen on board in June of 2008. She toured the ship and met crew members and passengers, and enjoyed lunch in the Caronia Restaurant, and for me to be the host on behalf of the ship's company was a great honour. It became very obvious as we toured the ship that Her Majesty has a huge affection and understanding for ships. One of the highlights was when we went on to the bridge wing, and QM2 was in further up river, and she was asked if she would blow our ship's whistle in return to the salute from QM2, which she enjoyed doing. But what really made my day was, as she was looking at QM2, her comments about the design of modern ships – and what she said will remain private between me and Her Majesty!

The last Royal visit was by HRH the Duke of Edinburgh on 11 November 2008, the day of the final call in Southampton before we sailed to Dubai. And what a day that was! The duke, a sailor himself of course, enjoyed his visit and lunched in the Princess Grill. Very soon it was time for departure, and the city of Southampton did us proud: fantastic fireworks, music, crowds on the shore all the way down river and hundreds of small boats around us – I don't think there was anybody who did not shed a tear that evening. It was a sad but glorious celebration of the ship and her long relationship with the port of Southampton.

Only days later we arrived in Dubai on 26 November, with a wonderful arrival salute from HMS Lancaster, who manned the side to salute QE2, the only time that has ever been done for a merchant ship. The next day, passengers disembarked and we handed the ship over to her new owners at a formal ceremony on the bridge where the Cunard House Flag, our paying off pennant and Red Ensign were lowered for the last time, and the flags of Dubai and Nakheel, the new owners, were raised.

I have to say, for me, and the other officers on the bridge wing, the staff captain, the chief engineer and the hotel manager, that was one of the most painful and heart-breaking moments of our lives. It really brought home that QE2 was gone, and no matter what they did to her thereafter, she would not be the QE2 we had known and loved all those years.

The modern ships have changed now to satisfy a new market and I can honestly say that we will never see the likes of her again. She will be sadly missed by all who sailed in her, both passengers and crew.

Queen Mary sailing on the North Atlantic Ocean. (Ian Boyle/Simplon Postcards)

Queen Mary seen here under the assistance of tugs. (Ian Boyle/Simplon Postcards)

Queen Mary held the speed record until 1952. (Ian Boyle/Simplon Postcards)

7

THE SECOND WORLD WAR

Built for the arts of peace and to link the Old World with the New, the Queens challenged the fury of Hitlerism in the Battle of the Atlantic. Without their aid the day of final victory must unquestionably have been postponed.

Sir Winston Churchill, 1946

The Second World War was to plunge Cunard-White Star back into armed conflict, with their ships once again at risk. At the outbreak of war, *Queen Mary* was safe in New York harbour, having just completed her 143rd crossing.

The decision was made in early 1940 that *Queen Elizabeth* had to leave Clydebank. In preparation for the voyage, the ship was painted all over in grey and given a degaussing coil to help her avoid damage from mines. Leaving the Clyde was a delicate process that required certain tidal conditions. As such, *Queen Elizabeth* had to wait until 26 February 1940 to make the journey to the Tail o' the Bank. The following day, the ship was handed over to her owners, despite not yet having had her sea trials.

It was widely believed that *Queen Elizabeth* would be sent to Southampton, where a fitting-out basin had been prepared for her. Winston Churchill, however, secretly ordered the ship to leave British waters, as she was a priority target for the Luftwaffe. The crew was not given a destination, but required to sign articles for an international voyage. Those unwilling to sign were detained until after the ship's sailing.

Sealed orders were sent to the ship, arriving on 2 March 1940, which were only to be opened once the ship was at sea. She sailed that day at 7.30 a.m., heading towards Northern Ireland. At 11 p.m. that same day Captain Townley opened the orders, discovering that his destination was New York.

The ship made a dash across the North Atlantic Ocean at 27.5 knots, her launching gear still attached, and arrived at her destination six days later. In New York she was berthed beside *Mauretania* and *Queen Mary*, as well as the French liner *Normandie*.

The ships were not to sit idle for long. Their size meant that they were ideal for trooping duties and as a result the British Admiralty soon requisitioned the Cunard-White Star ships for use in the war effort. *Mauretania* was sent to Sydney for conversion, departing New York on 20 March 1940. *Queen Mary* departed the following day for the same destination, via a different route.

One of the most terrible wartime losses was that of Cunard-White Star's *Lancastria*, which was sunk on 17 June 1940, whilst taking part in Operation Ariel. The loss of life was so great that the British Government banned announcement of the disaster, with the news taking five weeks to reach the public. There is no accurate record of how many people were aboard the ship when it sunk, though the number is estimated to be more than 6,000. Only 2,477 people were rescued from the wreck.

Queen Elizabeth sailed from New York for Singapore on 13 November 1940, to be converted to the world's largest troopship. Following her conversion, she joined *Mauretania*, *Aquitania* and *Queen Mary* in transporting Australian and New Zealand soldiers to the war zone.

The last of the White Star liners, *Britannic* and *Georgic*, were also called into service. *Britannic* had a very successful wartime career, and carried approximately 180,000 troops during the conflict.

Georgic did not enjoy the same luck. The Luftwaffe bombed her on 14 July 1941, whilst anchored at Port Tewfik, Suez. Her captain ordered her driven on to a reef so as not to block the harbour and she burned out. She was later refloated and sent to Harland & Wolff for an extensive refit and returned to military service, minus one funnel and with only a foremast.

After America entered the war, *Queen Elizabeth* and *Queen Mary* were given further refits to allow them to carry even more soldiers.

▶ DID YOU KNOW?

When *Queen Elizabeth* made her first transatlantic crossing, she still had her launching gear attached under the waterline.

They then commenced troop transporting duties, carrying American servicemen to Europe.

The events around the sinking of Cunard-White Star's *Laconia* were to forever change the operations of the German U-boat fleet. *Laconia* was torpedoed and sunk on 12 September 1942. She was carrying civilians and Italian prisoners of war, in addition to soldiers. Following the sinking, the U-boat captain and his crew commenced rescue operations, then proceeded to rendezvous with Vichy French ships, under the Red Cross banner, to transfer survivors.

Whilst underway, the U-boat was bombed by an American bomber. From this time on, the U-boat captains abandoned the practice of

Cunard's second *Mauretania* didn't sail for long in passenger service before the Second World War broke out. (Ian Boyle/Simplon Postcards)

Three Cunarders in convoy – *Queen Mary*, *Queen Elizabeth* and *Mauretania*. (Robert Henderson & Doug Cremer collection)

At the outbreak of the Second World War, the ocean became a battlefield once again and ships from all flags were destroyed. Cunard's fleet was a highly prized target for the Luftwaffe. (George Frame collection)

attempting to rescue civilian survivors under the 'Laconia Order'. This set the precedent for unrestricted submarine warfare, which devastated Allied shipping.

Queen Mary was involved in the sinking of another British ship in a tragic accident on 2 October 1942. The Queens were very effective troopships; carrying over 15,000 soldiers per voyage, but this also made them a very high priority target for unfriendly forces. As a result, both *Queen Mary* and *Queen Elizabeth* were under orders to steam at high speeds when crossing the Atlantic, and not to stop for any reason.

Queen Mary and *Queen Elizabeth* were both assigned naval escorts in an attempt to protect them, but the two ships were so fast that they often outstripped their escorts. On the day of the incident, *Queen Mary*'s escort was the light cruiser, HMS *Curacao*.

In an accidental manoeuvre, *Curacao* cut across *Queen Mary*'s path on their approach to Scotland. Due to the speed at which she was travelling, there was no time for *Queen Mary* to avoid the collision and she ploughed into the naval vessel, slicing the smaller vessel in half. The captain and officers were unable to stop to attempt to rescue survivors, and instead

Queen Mary continued on, with four other destroyer escorts pulling the survivors from the ocean.

In January 1945, the Cunard-White Star liner *Franconia* was selected as the base for the British delegation at the Yalta Conference. The purpose of this historic event, which took place between 4 February and 11 February, was to facilitate a meeting between Churchill, Roosevelt and Stalin, at which the three leaders discussed the post-war reorganisation of Europe.

With the 8 May 1945 unconditional surrender of Germany, the war in Europe was at an end. Cunard-White Star Line, as well as all other transatlantic shipping operators, was now faced with the mammoth task of repatriation and rebuilding.

The two largest troop carriers the world has ever seen, *Queen Mary* and *Queen Elizabeth*, had remained in military service as troopships for the duration of the war. At the end of the conflict they were hailed as national heroes. Their ability to carry such high numbers of troops on each crossing led to Winston Churchill remarking that they had shortened the length of the war by at least a year.

Escorts were sent to protect the troop ships; the Cunard Queens often outpaced the slower naval vessels. (George Frame collection)

Commodore Christopher Rynd reflects on his time at Cunard:

Cunard represents the tradition of grand ocean liners. It's about style, elegance and tradition. Its ships have interiors similar to those of the golden age of ocean travel and a tradition of service in a discrete yet friendly manner. There is a formality in both service and dress code that belongs here and it adds to the sense of occasion, especially in the evenings. Cunard staff exhibit a high level of professionalism in all we do.

I am honoured to be commodore of such a fleet, its senior master. Cunard ships attract attention wherever they go and thus we are involved in events. For example, most recently all three vessels rendezvoused in Lisbon at the end of their world voyages and berthed all together at a new facility, then sailed in formation down river and later in line abreast at sea. It was a rare sight.

In Southampton, the 10th anniversary of QM2's naming by HM the Queen was celebrated with a rendezvous of all three vessels in a bow-to-bow formation on arrival, with whistles sounded and flags waved. Later there was a celebratory luncheon in the presence of HRH the Duke of Edinburgh and fireworks before all three sailed together that evening. It was a thrilling day for all on board.

In Liverpool we arrived on the very day another great ocean liner, *Aquitania*, sailed on her maiden voyage exactly 100 years before,

British losses were high during the war, with both civilian and military ships lost. (George Frame collection)

acknowledging that great Cunard liner and Cunard's spiritual home of Liverpool, where the grand Cunard Building stands on the river's edge. We sailed to wonderful send-off by a large crowd with music and the waving of flags.

Our fleet of three liners is a good size. It allows exclusivity both for our guests and for the ship's company or crew. They have a sense of this and there is a feeling of belonging, of being shipmates or colleagues, with this great group of people. That reinforces what we are and all we do.

One of the greatest pleasures of the job is the people element. In meeting our guests the officers and I help enable that friendly mixing of like-minded people, even though many guests come from different places, a cosmopolitan mix, which is another enjoyable factor that makes the social mix more interesting. Behind the scenes, meeting the crew in the course of various rounds, inspections and meetings reinforces that sense of being shipmates, a team. Also running in the background is developing professionalism and being as safe an operation as we possibly can be.

We celebrate our 175th Anniversary in 2015. A great endorsement of the company and its brand is that is has not only survived but it has maintained this reputation of style, service and safety. It's wonderful to belong to that and have the privilege of being part of the team that carries this company into the future.

,

Queen Elizabeth commenced her career as a troop ship. (Michael Pocock/Maritime Quest)

Mauretania was used for trooping duties. (George Frame collection)

Lancastria was sunk, resulting in a shocking loss of life. (Ian Boyle/Simplon Postcards)

Left: Cunard-White Star's *Georgic* was bombed by the Luftwaffe. (George Frame collection)

Below: Cunard's *Queen Mary* as a troopship. This image was taken in Sydney Harbour. (Robert Henderson & Doug Cremer collection)

Queen Mary painted grey as a troop vessel. (Robert Henderson & Doug Cremer collection)

In this wartime view, *Queen Elizabeth* is carrying over 10,000 troops. (Robert Henderson & Doug Cremer collection)

Queen Elizabeth in Sydney harbour. (Robert Henderson & Doug Cremer collection)

▶ **DID YOU KNOW?**

All four of Cunard's large express liners – *Queen Elizabeth*, *Queen Mary*, *Mauretania* and *Aquitania* – survived service in the Second World War.

Queen Mary's troops as the ship prepares to depart. (Robert Henderson & Doug Cremer collection)

S.S. QUEEN MARY & QUEEN ELIZABETH FROM THE AIR.

Above right: *Queen Mary* in her wartime colours. (Ian Boyle/ Simplon Postcards)

Above: *Queen Mary* passes her restored sister, *Queen Elizabeth*, at the end of their military service. (Ian Boyle/ Simplon Postcards)

The two Queens at the end of their wartime service. *Queen Elizabeth* (left) painted in civilian colours while *Queen Mary* (right) retains her wartime grey. (Ian Boyle/ Simplon Postcards)

8

POST-WAR RECOVERY

Getting there is half the fun.

Cunard advertising slogan from the 1950s

The Allied victory in Europe meant that Cunard-White Star's requisitioned tonnage was no longer required for the dangerous and highly demanding trooping operation. However, Cunard-White Star did not immediately regain use of their ships.

Cunard-White Star's four largest liners, *Queen Mary*, *Queen Elizabeth*, *Mauretania* and *Aquitania*, were used for several months to repatriate American and Canadian soldiers and their brides. The additional service meant that it took some time before Cunard-White Star was in a position to resume their Atlantic express service.

Queen Elizabeth was the first to be released from government service. She was returned to Clydebank where she was fitted out for the first time as a passenger ship and finally received and passed her builders' sea trials. *Queen Mary* was released from service in September 1946. She was given an extensive refit where she was reconditioned to her pre-war glory.

With their two express liners in commercial service Cunard-White Star was able to finally commence the world's first two-ship weekly transatlantic service. *Queen Mary* and *Queen Elizabeth* proved very popular with the travelling public. The ships were fast and reliable and the Cunard-White Star service was, for a time, the quickest and most luxurious way to travel the North Atlantic.

Once again the other European lines had been decimated by the war, leaving little competition for Cunard-White Star on the express service. Cunard-White Star was also running other services with their restored intermediate liners, and ex-express liners.

Aquitania had once again survived the war and re-entered Cunard-White Star service in 1946, being then chartered by the Canadian Government to transport war brides and their children to Canada. She remained in this role until 1949, when she was laid up as she was too costly to refit to new safety standards.

Mauretania, which had entered service just prior to the outbreak of the Second World War, was able to resume her Atlantic service in 1947, after extensive refurbishment at her builders, Cammell Laird & Co.

The last of the White Star liners, *Britannic* and *Georgic*, returned to passenger services, with *Britannic*'s first peacetime passenger voyage occurring in 1948. *Georgic*'s wartime foundering meant that she was never quite the same again, with the ship plagued by heavy vibrations from the extensive and hasty rebuilding effort. She was managed and operated by Cunard-White Star, running services for the Ministry of Transport.

While *Britannic* was placed on the prestigious Liverpool to New York services, *Georgic* was used for the immigrant trade between the UK and Australia and New Zealand, under the assisted passage scheme. *Georgic* resumed transatlantic services in 1950 and was laid up in 1954, having been used as a troopship in the Korean War. Following this, she briefly re-entered service on the Australian passage before being laid up again.

Cunard was soon to supplement their fleet with new post-war tonnage. *Parthia* and *Media* entered service for Cunard in 1947. These ships were designed and built as combination cargo and passenger ships. Each ship had room for 250 first-class passengers, in addition to their cargo-carrying capacity. The privacy afforded by having such a small passenger complement meant that they became quite popular with travelling celebrities, who often found it difficult to keep up appearances on larger liners such as the Queens.

In 1947, the company became known as Cunard Line once again, after Cunard bought out White Star Line's interest in the organisation. Despite the name change, the White Star pennant continued to be flown from the aft mast aboard the two remaining White Star ships, *Britannic* and *Georgic*, until each ship's retirement. Furthermore, both liners retained their White Star livery and buff-coloured funnels.

On 30 October 1947, Cunard's Green Goddess, *Caronia*, was launched in a ceremony presided over by HRH Princess Elizabeth. This was the princess' last official engagement before her marriage to Prince Philip. A dual-purpose ship, *Caronia* earned her nickname due to being painted in four shades of green, rather than the traditional Cunard matt black hull with white superstructure. This colour scheme was purposely chosen to signify that this ship was designed for cruising and gave her an instantly recognisable and unique identity.

To satisfy the dual-purpose design, *Caronia* maintained the traditional ocean liner traits of speed, strength and stability. However, *Caronia* was completed with several features making her suitable for cruising. She had large picture windows, affording excellent views of cruising destinations, while a large outdoor swimming pool and lido area allowed passengers to enjoy the outdoors while the ship was cruising in the tropics.

Queen Elizabeth held the record as the world's largest passenger ship until 1996 when she was finally eclipsed by *Carnival Destiny*. (Ian Boyle/Simplon Postcards)

Queen Mary makes way from New York Harbour in her peacetime livery. (Ian Boyle/Simplon Postcards)

With her twin funnels and clutter-free decks, *Queen Elizabeth* makes for an impressive sight. (Ian Boyle/Simplon Postcards)

Cunard's new flagship and the world's largest liner, *Queen Elizabeth*. (Ian Boyle/Simplon Postcards)

The *Queen Mary* at sea. (Ian Boyle/Simplon Postcards)

Caronia entered service in January 1949, with a maiden voyage across the Atlantic. After several more Atlantic crossings, she made her first cruise voyage to the Caribbean that same year and carved out a reputation of excellence, attracting a loyal following for the remainder of her career.

Aside from the primary transatlantic liners, other liners, such as the 1923 built *Franconia* and her sisters *Scythia* and *Samaria*, were returned to passenger service. Having been built as replacement tonnage for ships lost during the First World War, these three ships survived the Second World War and, following repatriation duties, were utilised by Cunard on supplementary transatlantic voyages throughout the 1950s until their retirement.

In 1951, Cunard acquired further cargo tonnage when they purchased the 1948-built *Silverplane* and *Silverbriar* from the Silver Line. Renamed *Alsatia* and *Andria*, the combination liners were converted into dedicated freighters, remaining in Cunard service until 1963.

In 1952, *Queen Mary* lost her title as holder of the transatlantic speed records when the United States Lines introduced their new flagship, SS *United States*. The American Government wanted a large liner that could be used as a troop ship, should the need arise, and, as a result, built

> " Caroline Scallan was the head of Cunard's enrichment programme and booked many famous people to speak aboard Cunard's fleet:
>
> Cunard is one of the most recognisable brands. Working at Cunard was a privilege. I always felt like I was part of something really special – watching historic moments from ship launches, royal visits and guests enjoying the unique White Star Service offered aboard Cunard's ships. "

Queen Elizabeth as seen from the air. Note the wash from the propellers as the mighty liner berths. (Ian Boyle/Simplon Postcards)

an extremely fast ship. Cunard considered refurbishing *Queen Elizabeth* in order to recapture the record; however, *United States'* average speed of 34 knots was unbeatable.

In 1953, *Media* received a refit, which included the introduction of fin stabilisers aboard. This refit was so successful that the technology was later rolled out to other Cunard liners.

Alsatia and *Andria* were soon joined by new-build cargo vessels, including *Pavia* and *Phrygia*. Built in Glasgow by William Hamilton & Co., they entered service for Cunard in 1953 and 1955 respectively. These 3,500-ton vessels operated cargo services for Cunard until they were sold in 1965.

In 1954, the *Saxonia*-class liners were introduced on to the Canadian service. Four near-identical sisters, each ship grossed approximately 21,600 tons. The fleet, comprising *Saxonia*, *Ivernia*, *Carinthia* and *Sylvania*, proved popular on the route and enjoyed a successful early career with Cunard.

By the time the *Saxonia*-class liners entered service, the transatlantic landscape was starting to change. BOAC commenced transatlantic Comet 4 services in 1958, which was followed by the far more successful Boeing 707 and Douglas DC-8. These jet services were about to change Cunard forever.

Cunard's *Queen Elizabeth* being handled by tugboats. (Ian Boyle/Simplon Postcards)

Queen Elizabeth being handled by the tugs. (Ian Boyle/Simplon Postcards)

Queen Elizabeth, then the world's largest liner. (Robert Henderson & Doug Cremer collection)

The Cunard Line flagship arrives in Cunard's British hub at Southampton. (Ian Boyle/Simplon Postcards)

Passers-by catch a glimpse of *Queen Mary*. (Ian Boyle/Simplon Postcards)

Queen Elizabeth docked at the end of another crossing. (Ian Boyle/Simplon Postcards)

Queen Elizabeth passes New York. (Ian Boyle/Simplon Postcards)

Queen Elizabeth on a perfect ocean. (Ian Boyle/Simplon Postcards)

Queen Elizabeth picking up speed as she heads out to sea. (Ian Boyle/Simplon Postcards)

Queen Mary departs on another transatlantic voyage. (Ian Boyle/Simplon Postcards)

Queen Mary on a still ocean. (Ian Boyle/Simplon Postcards)

Mauretania shared many features with *Queen Elizabeth*. (Ian Boyle/Simplon Postcards)

Mauretania was smaller than the Queens yet still a popular ship. (Ian Boyle/Simplon Postcards)

Mauretania's (pictured) intended sister was redesigned into the *Caronia*. (Ian Boyle/Simplon Postcards)

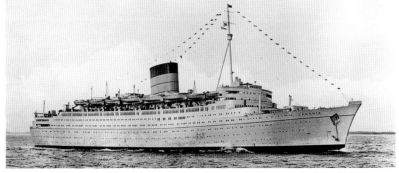

Cunard opted to paint *Caronia* in a green livery that led to her nickname of the Green Goddess. (Ian Boyle/Simplon Postcards)

Caronia was Cunard's first purpose-built cruise ship. (Ian Boyle/Simplon Postcards)

Caronia was unique in her design, with the widest funnel at sea and a single mast. (Ian Boyle/Simplon Postcards)

Caronia was painted in four shades of green, giving her a distinctive appearance. (Ian Boyle/Simplon Postcards)

Caronia on another cruise with flags flying and anchor dropped. (Ian Boyle/Simplon Postcards)

Her cruising role took *Caronia* to exotic destinations. (Ian Boyle/Simplon Postcards)

Media was popular with celebrities due to her intimate nature. (Ian Boyle/Simplon Postcards)

Pathia was small and private, enticing to celebrities. (Ian Boyle/Simplon Postcards)

An artist's impression of the new *Saxonia*. (Ian Boyle/Simplon Postcards)

▶ **DID YOU KNOW?**

The Queens used nearly 1,000 tons of fuel per day on the transatlantic run.

Saxonia was the class leader for the *Saxonia* sisters. (Ian Boyle/Simplon Postcards)

Saxonia en route to Canada. (Ian Boyle/Simplon Postcards)

When times got tough, Cunard sent their ships cruising. Here we see *Franconia* in her post-cruising guise. (Ian Boyle/Simplon Postcards)

Carmania (ex-*Saxonia*) in *Caronia*-inspired green livery. (Ian Boyle/Simplon Postcards)

▶ **DID YOU KNOW?** . . . .

While the *Saxonia*-class liners had luxurious first-class accommodation, their tourist class was well behind the times. The accommodation was small and most cabins did not have private bathrooms.

Carmania and *Franconia* were treated to significant refurbishments, including a paint scheme similar to *Caronia*'s for their cruising role. (Ian Boyle/Simplon Postcards)

Queen Mary at the Ocean Terminal, Southampton. (Ian Boyle/Simplon Postcards)

There is no more impressive a sight than a Queen at sea. This image depicts *Queen Elizabeth*. (Ian Boyle/Simplon Postcards)

Queen Elizabeth was truly majestic. This image is of the Cunard flagship at Southampton. (Ian Boyle/Simplon Postcards)

9

THE AGE OF
THE JET

Flying is a fad.

An unnamed Cunard director

In 1957, even before commercial jet services became commonplace, for the first time more passengers crossed the Atlantic by air than by ocean liner.

Cunard's transatlantic passenger numbers had been reducing over the previous years, since the introduction of regular airliner services on the Lockheed Constellation and Douglas DC-4, while the British-built Comet 4 offered the first transatlantic jet services; albeit on a relatively small scale. With the introduction of Boeing's immensely popular 707, the era of the transatlantic liner was coming to an end. Passengers flocked to the airlines and the diminished passenger numbers meant that many of Cunard's ships were no longer suitable for their current roles.

Scythia was scrapped in 1958, having become the longest-serving Cunarder to that date; *Georgic* was scrapped in 1956, and *Britannic* in 1960, effectively ending the White Star Line. In 1961, both *Media* and *Parthia* left the Cunard fleet, sold to other shipping companies.

Cunard had been planning a new ship, codenamed Q3, which was to be an updated version of their current Queens. However, on 19 October 1961, these plans were abandoned. Cunard could not justify building another ship of similar dimensions when their current ships were losing profitability. Instead they began to consider new options.

Mauretania was converted for cruising in 1962, undergoing an extensive refurbishment and being repainted in varying shades of green, to match *Caronia*. *Ivernia* and *Saxonia* were also given cruising refits, with both ships having their aft decks altered to add a swimming pool and lido area. Following their refits they were renamed *Franconia* and *Carmania*.

Also in 1962, Cunard entered into a joint venture agreement with the British Overseas Airways Corporation to form BOAC-Cunard. This subsidiary airline operated flights from the UK to North America and the tropics.

In 1965, *Queen Elizabeth* was given a refit, with air conditioning installed and her aft decks modified to include a lido deck and swimming pool, much like the refits given to other ships. It was hoped that this refit would allow *Queen Elizabeth* to perform a dual-purpose role – cruising and transatlantic line voyage. Unfortunately, *Queen Elizabeth* proved too large for such a purpose.

Queen Mary was also sent cruising in the quieter months, but without the additional changes that *Queen Elizabeth* had been given she proved even less successful as a cruise ship. Both *Queen Mary* and *Queen Elizabeth* were too large to transit the Panama Canal, seriously restricting their ability to visit different ports. They both also had deep draughts, which meant that they were unable to enter the shallower ports of the Caribbean and Mediterranean, further restricting their cruising capabilities.

On 30 December 1964, it had been announced that John Brown & Co. of Clydebank, Scotland had won the tender to build Cunard's latest ocean liner. Codenamed Q4, this ship was to be smaller than the *Queen Mary* and *Queen Elizabeth*. She was to be built as a dual-purpose liner, with dimensions small enough to enable her to transit the Panama Canal, and a draught shallow enough to allow her to enter most cruising ports. Her keel was laid down on 5 July 1965. The building of this new ship was partially financed by the British Government on the understanding that

the ship be built in the UK. The rest of the finance came from mortgaging eleven of Cunard's existing ships.

In November 1965, *Mauretania* was retired. She had been making losses and Cunard could no longer maintain her in her role. She was sold for scrap, departing Southampton on 20 November 1965.

Attempts were made to transform other Cunard ships into part-time cruise ships. *Sylvania* was given a refurbishment for cruising in 1965, though this was not as extensive as the refits her sister ships had received years before. As a result, she was less successful in her new role than they. The fourth of the *Saxonia* sisters, *Carinthia*, was given a partial cruising refit later that decade but again, as it was not complete the refit did not greatly extend the ship's life with Cunard.

BOAC bought out Cunard's share of the BOAC-Cunard joint venture in 1966. This freed up more capital for Cunard, though it was not enough to halt the requirement to sell tonnage to fund their new build. On 8 May 1967, the captains of *Queen Mary* and *Queen Elizabeth* learned the fate of their ships whilst at sea. Both ships were to become floating hotels in America.

Mauretania was sent cruising before she was sold for scrap. (Ian Boyle/Simplon Postcards)

Farewell to the great *Queen Mary*. (Ian Boyle/Simplon Postcards)

On 20 September 1967, Q4 was officially launched. HM Queen Elizabeth II presided over the ceremony, naming the ship *Queen Elizabeth the Second*. As there was already a Royal Naval vessel with the name *Queen Elizabeth II*, Cunard applied to Buckingham Palace, receiving permission to name their new vessel *Queen Elizabeth 2*, using the number 2, rather than the Roman numeral, to distinguish the two ships.

Queen Mary's departure from the Cunard fleet happened later that year. She sailed from Southampton for the final time on 31 October, bound for California. The voyage was her longest ever peacetime voyage, with the ship going via Cape Horn.

With fitting out and engine troubles, *Queen Elizabeth 2* took almost a further two years before she entered service. During that time, more ships left the Cunard fleet. In 1968, *Caronia* was withdrawn from service and sold to Star Shipping. *Carinthia* and *Sylvania* were both sold to the Sitmar Line, where they were given full cruising refits and remained in service under their new names, *Fairsea* and *Fairwind*, until 2005 and 2004 respectively.

Queen Elizabeth also departed the Cunard fleet that year. She was renamed *Elizabeth* and plans were created for her to become a floating hotel in Fort Lauderdale, in a joint venture between Cunard and a group

▶ DID YOU KNOW?

Seawise University (the former *Queen Elizabeth*) never opened as a university. Prior to the completion of her conversion, several fires broke out aboard and she burnt out and sank in Hong Kong harbour.

Queen Elizabeth briefly opened as an attraction at Fort Lauderdale. (Ian Boyle/Simplon Postcards)

Number 736's bulbous bow. (Cunard/Michael Gallagher)

The great bow of Number 736, awaiting launch. (Cunard/ Michael Gallagher)

Launched and named *Queen Elizabeth 2*, she is seen here at the fitting-out basin. (Cunard/Michael Gallagher)

QE2's mast was very stylish. (Cunard/Michael Gallagher)

QE2's mast being attached atop the bridge. (Cunard/Michael Gallagher)

Cunard's new flagship, *Queen Elizabeth 2*. (Cunard/Michael Gallagher)

The Grill Room aboard *QE2* had sculptures that dominated the décor. (Cunard/Michael Gallagher)

QE2 on sea trials. (Cunard/Michael Gallagher)

of Philadelphia businessmen. Never officially converted, the ship lingered in Fort Lauderdale, opening briefly as a hotel in her original format. The lack of funds meant the plans fell through fairly quickly. She was sold in 1970 to C.Y. Tung, a Hong Kong businessman, for conversion to a floating university in Hong Kong under the name of *Seawise University*.

After a much-delayed fit-out programme, in which boiler malfunctions had plagued the new liner, *Queen Elizabeth 2* finally departed on her maiden voyage on 30 May 1969. The new ship had a very different exterior profile, with a single, stylised mast and a thin white-and-black funnel, without the traditional Cunard red. Internally she was modern, with interior spaces that made use of chrome, aluminium, fibreglass and leather. A two-class ship during her transatlantic crossings, she operated as a single-class ship for cruises.

QE2, as the new ship became affectionately known, proved very popular, and became the longest lasting of the dual-purpose liners that were introduced at the time. In fact, she was so popular that Cunard were able to start repaying the government loan they had acquired for her construction.

The Columbia Restaurant aboard *QE2* was for first-class passengers. (Cunard/Michael Gallagher)

Above and below: The Lookout Bar aboard *QE2* was the only forward facing bar aboard the ship, and sported a very 'swinging 60s' decor. (Cunard/Michael Gallagher)

QE2's Lookout Bar was radical in its design. (Cunard/Michael Gallagher)

The Britannia restaurant was *QE2*'s tourist-class dining room. (Cunard/Michael Gallagher)

QE2's Double Down Room sported a spiral staircase, double height and a large dance floor. (Cunard/Michael Gallagher)

With black walls, chrome balustrades and green leather chairs, *QE2*'s Midships Lobby was futuristic and modern. (Cunard/Michael Gallagher)

The Queens Room was *QE2*'s first-class lounge. (Cunard/Michael Gallagher)

The *QE2* was both a liner and a cruise ship, and is seen here berthed during a cruise. (Cunard/Michael Gallagher)

Below: *QE2* at rest during a cruise. (Cunard/Michael Gallagher)

▶ **DID YOU KNOW?**

In 1974, *Caribia*, the former *Caronia*, was sold for scrap, having been mostly laid up since her withdrawal from Cunard. During the voyage under tow to Taiwan, *Caribia* was wrecked off the coast of Guam.

10

TRAFALGAR HOUSE OWNERSHIP

Cunard's cruising activity is complementary to [our] Caribbean hotel developments.

Trafalgar House statement on the purchase of Cunard Line

With the *QE2* settled into regular service, Cunard set about streamlining the business further in order to allow them to repay the government loan. *QE2* proved to be a very popular ship. The new *Queen* was a vast departure from traditional Cunard liners; and was very popular with younger ocean travellers.

Seven years prior to *QE2*'s entry into service, the Trafalgar House Co., a fledgling property development firm, was establishing itself in London. Under the leadership of a young Sir Nigel Broakes, the organisation grew quickly and by the early 1970s the London Stock Exchange-listed company was acquiring a variety of assets. As part of its seemingly unstoppable expansion, Trafalgar House acquired Cunard Line in 1971. With the acquisition came the Cunard fleet, which included *QE2*, *Franconia* and *Carmania*, as well as a cargo fleet of over forty vessels.

At the time of the acquisition, Cunard also had two 14,000-ton cruise ships on order. Originally designed as the first two of eight vessels for Overseas National Airways, the *Cunard Adventurer* and *Cunard Ambassador*

entered service in 1971 and 1972 respectively. With the anticipated arrival of the new tonnage, *Franconia* and *Carmania* were withdrawn from service. This saw a brief end to Cunard's dedicated presence in the Caribbean.

Since 1967 Cunard had contributed to the joint-venture container line, ACL. As part of their commitment to this collaboration, the line operated two of ACL's roll-on roll-off container ships. These vessels, *Atlantic Conveyor* and *Atlantic Causeway*, each carried wheeled vehicles as well as containers and were built by Swan Hunter in Newcastle upon Tyne.

With the exception of the ACL venture, Trafalgar House moved to divest the Cunard freight business, leaving Cunard to concentrate on passenger operations. *QE2* was given a £1 million refurbishment in 1972, which included the addition of balcony suites to her signal and sun decks. This made *QE2* one of the first passenger ships to offer balcony cabins.

QE2 was the subject of a bomb scare in 1972 while on an eastbound transatlantic crossing. Following a telephoned threat, the ship's security team, under the command of Captain Law, swept the vessel and found nothing. Nevertheless, the threat was taken seriously, and a team of highly trained members of the British SAS were parachuted into the sea near QE2. Once aboard the ship, they performed their own search and found nothing. The event turned out to be a hoax and the culprit was later arrested for making similar threats to American Airlines.

In 1975, QE2 undertook her maiden world cruise. Her dual-purpose design made her the perfect vessel for long-distance cruising, while the 963ft length of the ship meant that, unlike the previous Queens, QE2 could transit the Panama Canal. The ninety-two-day voyage saw QE2 visit twenty-three ports and complete her first full circumnavigation of the globe.

Cunard's Trafalgar years were characterised by expansion of services across a diverse range of markets. The first major step in this programme was the acquisition of further tonnage. Two new 17,000-ton cruise ships, each with the capacity to carry over 940 passengers, were added to the fleet in the mid-1970s. Named *Cunard Countess* and *Cunard Princess*, the vessels were originally designed with input from *Playboy* founder Hugh Heffner. Intended to be floating playgrounds, the ships were to sail for the MGM brand.

With Cunard's acquisition of the ships during the building process, their design was tweaked to become two of the most successful early 4-star cruise ships. From 1976, Cunard positioned the *Cunard Countess* in the Caribbean, while *Cunard Princess* entered service in 1977 and concentrated mainly on the Mediterranean service, as well as occasional voyages to Bermuda and Alaska.

In 1982, four ships in Cunard's fleet were requisitioned for use during the Falklands War. This included QE2, which was requisitioned on 3 May. The QE2 was at sea when the announcement was made and the ship's captain and officers actually heard about the ship's requisition via BBC Radio 2 before they were officially advised by Cunard.

QE2's transformation for wartime use was dramatic, with the ship's aft decks being cut away for helicopter use; while her decks were strengthened with the addition of steel plating. At the end of the eight-day refurbishment, QE2 set sail for the South Atlantic. Aboard the ship were 3,000 troops from the 5th Infantry Brigade, as well as the Welsh Guards and Gurkhas.

During the campaign, QE2 was purposely kept out of the warzone, staying in the relative safety of Cumberland Bay. There, she transferred her troops to other ships, including the P&O liner *Canberra*. QE2 then took on survivors from the HMS *Ardent*, HMS *Coventry* and HMS *Antelope*

before sailing back to Southampton. The ship arrived at Southampton on 11 June 1982 and was met by the Royal Yacht *Britannia* with HM the Queen Mother aboard who sent QE2 a special message of congratulations.

The Cunard-operated ACL vessels *Atlantic Conveyor* and *Atlantic Causeway* were also requisitioned for use during the Falklands War. They were particularly useful for the war effort due to their unique design as both container ship and roll-on roll-off carrier. Both ships were used to carry RAF helicopters and Sea Harriers as well as vehicles and cargo supplies for the war effort. While *Atlantic Causeway* successfully returned home at the end of the campaign, *Atlantic Conveyor* was not so lucky. She was attacked on 25 May by an Argentine Dassault-Breguet Super Étendard jet, which fired two Exocet missiles into the ship. She burnt out with the loss of twelve crewmembers, including her captain. She was later taken under tow but sunk shortly afterwards.

At the end of the conflict in October 1982, the *Cunard Countess* was requisitioned for use by the government. She was used for troop movements between Ascension Island and Port Stanley while the airfield was repaired from damage sustained during the conflict. *Cunard Countess* also undertook a special voyage carrying families of those lost during the war to the South Atlantic for a commemorative ceremony.

At the end of their service, each of the surviving Cunard ships was given an extensive refit; QE2's was undertaken in Southampton and included the addition of the first Golden Door Spa at Sea. *Cunard Countess'* refit contract was awarded to a shipyard in Malta, which caused an outcry among nationalists in Great Britain.

In 1983, Cunard's fleet was again expanded when Trafalgar House purchased Norwegian America Line. The purchase included two of the highest-rated ships afloat: *Sagafjord* and *Vistafjord*. Both were renowned among 5-star travellers, and boasted a fiercely loyal clientele. After considering renaming the ships to re-establish the traditional 'ia' naming convention, it was decided to retain their Norwegian names, as well as their Norwegian crew.

With their funnels repainted in the Cunard colours and initially operating under the Cunard-NAL sub-brand, *Sagafjord* and *Vistafjord* settled into a regular cruising schedule. *Sagafjord* undertook annual world cruises while *Vistafjord*'s itineraries concentrated mainly on the European luxury cruise market.

Trafalgar House further expanded Cunard's fleet in 1986, when the company purchased the ailing Sea Goddess Line. Sea Goddess had run into financial hardship after completing the first two luxury yachts in what was to be a series of eight ships. With this acquisition, Cunard formed the Cunard-Sea Goddess sub-brand and placed these two highly rated ships into service.

That same year, QE2's service-life expectancy was extended with a mammoth reengineering project. The ship's steam turbines had been troublesome since she entered service and by the mid-1980s were creating significant issues for the ship. Thus, US$100 million was spent on what was the largest and most complex marine propulsion transformation programme in history.

The works, which were completed at the Lloyd Werft shipyard in Bremerhaven, Germany, included the removal of QE2's entire steam propulsion system, which amounted to 4,700 tons of material. This was replaced with an entirely new diesel electric system comprising nine medium-speed MAN-B&W engines, each weighing 220 tons.

The ship's funnel was removed to facilitate the removal of her old power plant as well as the installation of the new engines. These diesels created power, which fed two gigantic British-built propulsion motors – the largest ever constructed for a merchant vessel.

During QE2's refurbishment programme, Sagafjord replaced her on the transatlantic crossings, maintaining Cunard's regular presence on this route. Sagafjord proved very popular on this route, and her voyages enjoyed strong bookings.

QE2 returned to commercial service in April 1987, with her first voyage being a short trip along the Solent. Aboard was HRH Princess Diana along with a group of local underprivileged children.

In 1989, a group of Japanese businessmen chartered the Cunard flagship twice. The first charter was for seventy-five days, in honour of the 130th anniversary of the city of Yokohama. The second lasted six months, with QE2 docked in Osaka for the World Exposition. During QE2's charters, Vistafjord was used as Cunard's transatlantic liner. Vistafjord had originally been built with transatlantic crossings in mind, and her use in this role proved popular both with passengers and her crew. Vistafjord also offered

QE2 departing New York in her original colour scheme. (Cunard/Michael Gallagher)

CAPTAIN LAW'S ADDRESS TO QE2 PASSENGERS DURING THE 1972 BOMB SCARE

Ladies and Gentlemen, we have received information concerning a threat of a bomb-explosion on board this ship some time during this voyage.

We have received such threats in the past, which have so far turned out to be hoaxes. However, we always take them seriously and take every possible precaution.

On this occasion we are being assisted by the British Government who are sending out bomb disposal experts who will be parachuted into the sea and picked up by boat and brought aboard.

I will of course keep you fully informed about the situation. Cunard are taking every precaution ashore and on board and will take any necessary action to minimise risk. If there is any question of it being necessary to pay over money, this will be done ashore in New York.

I can only ask you to remain calm. On these occasions lots of rumours tend to circulate.

Please only take notice of any information that comes from me directly or from one of my officers. That is all for the moment.

unique itineraries, including a voyage to the Amazon, and a forty-day cruise to the Mediterranean, which departed from the American cruising hub of Fort Lauderdale.

The beginning of the 1990s was characterised by further expansion. Trafalgar House added European river vessels, including the renowned *Mozart* and *Dresden*, to the Cunard stable, as well as hotel management. In fact, Cunard were operating the Ritz Hotel in London for Trafalgar House.

In 1993, Cunard's fleet expanded again with a joint venture with the Crown Cruise Line. Crown had been operating three new ships, which now sailed as *Cunard Crown Monarch*, *Cunard Crown Jewel* and *Cunard Crown Dynasty* under the Cunard-Crown sub-brand. *Cunard Countess* and *Cunard Princess* were moved under the Cunard-Crown banner, although their original names were retained.

While *Cunard Crown Jewel* and *Cunard Crown Dynasty* were popular ships, the line made an error in sending *Cunard Crown Monarch* to Australia. Australian cruising had been dominated by Sitmar's (later P&O Holidays) *Fairstar* for many years. *Fairstar* offered cheap, informal cruises from Sydney to the South Pacific, which was perfect for the fledgling Australian cruise market. *Cunard Crown Monarch*'s more sophisticated and expensive voyages were unappealing to the local market at the time and the ship was withdrawn and sold in 1994.

That year saw the final Trafalgar House-controlled addition to the Cunard fleet. *Royal Viking Sun* was the flagship of the Royal Viking Line, which Trafalgar acquired and merged with Cunard. The line created yet another sub-brand, Cunard Royal Viking, which operated *Royal Viking Sun* along with *Sagafjord* and *Vistafjord*. The addition of *Royal Viking* meant Cunard's passenger fleet reached its largest size since the introduction of the jet. However, the mismatched fleet, sprawling hotel and river-cruise operation was difficult to control, expensive to market and ultimately unprofitable.

Trafalgar House took a number of steps to try and stem the losses at Cunard. These included a restructure of the line, as well as a multi-million-pound refurbishment of *QE2* in order to revitalise her public areas. While *QE2*'s refit resulted in a dramatic and ultimately very popular transformation of the liner, the work aboard the ship overran the schedule with construction still underway when *QE2* sailed on her December 1994 voyage. This was a public relations disaster for the line as the negative press associated with the voyage lasted well into the new year.

By the end of *QE2*'s 1995 world cruise her reputation had been restored; however, Cunard's finances kept deteriorating. During that year the line posted a £16 million loss. This resulted in a further restructure of the line, which included the ageing *Sagafjord* being flagged for retirement from Cunard service in 1996. *Sagafjord* had not enjoyed the same care as *Vistafjord* and had missed several scheduled refurbishments, which had impacted on her 5-star plus rating. Her removal from the fleet had been expected for several months before the official announcement was made. Other tonnage departed during 1995, including *Cunard Princess* and *Cunard Crown Jewel*, which were both sold, leaving the Cunard Crown fleet diminished to just two ships.

The cost of maintaining sub-brands took a further toll on Cunard's finances and by 1997 *Cunard Countess* and *Cunard Crown Dynasty* had also left the fleet.

By 1998, Cunard's fleet had been reduced to five ships. The mismatched fleet was plagued by the company's lack of funds. Trafalgar House had by this time been acquired by Kværner, which sought a buyer for the ailing company.

Cunard Adventurer and *Cunard Ambassador* were used for cruising. (Bill Miller)

Cunard Adventurer berthed during a cruise. (Tee Adams)

Looking up at *QE2*'s original funnel. (Tee Adams)

An aerial shot of the world's most iconic floating resort, *QE2*. (Cunard/Michael Gallagher)

Cunard Princess was originally to be named 'Cunard Conquest'. (Tee Adams)

Rob Lightbody runs the well-known *QE2* Story website and has had a long connection with Cunard's longest serving flagship:

For years, in the 1970s and '80s, my dad would disappear off to faraway lands 'to fix the *QE2*'. We knew what she was – she was famous and on TV often – but I didn't truly understand what she was until I went aboard, first as a child, then as an adult. She was the most special, amazing, beautiful ship in the world. The seven seas are a bit less interesting without *QE2* sailing upon them.

▶ **DID YOU KNOW?**
....

Royal Viking Sun did not stay with Seabourn for long. In 2002, she was moved to Holland America and was renamed *Prinsendam*.

Left: *Cunard Countess* was Cunard's Caribbean cruise ship. (Ronald W. Warwick; *QE2: The Cunard Flagship Queen Elizabeth 2*)

QE2 refuels at sea during her service in the Falklands War. (Ronald W. Warwick; *QE2: The Cunard Flagship Queen Elizabeth 2*)

Above: A sea king helicopter departs from *QE2*'s aft decks during the Falklands War. (Ronald W. Warwick; *QE2: The Cunard Flagship Queen Elizabeth 2*)

QE2's bow was converted into a helipad for her service in the Falklands War. (Ronald W. Warwick; *QE2: The Cunard Flagship Queen Elizabeth 2*)

Left: *QE2* in Philadelphia in April 1982, shortly before her Falklands service. The Walt Whitman bridge, between Pennsylvania and New Jersey, can be seen behind, as well as a Curtis Bay tug. (Tee Adams)

Below: *QE2* undergoes her post-war refurbishment. (Ronald W. Warwick; *QE2: The Cunard Flagship Queen Elizabeth 2*)

Upon returning to Southampton, *QE2* was greeted by Queen Elizabeth, The Queen Mother aboard the Royal Yacht *Britannia*. (Cunard/Michael Gallagher)

QE2 in her grey hull, her post-war colour scheme. (Tee Adams)

Looking somewhat awkward, QE2 is seen here in her short-lived pebble grey livery. (Ronald W. Warwick; QE2: The Cunard Flagship Queen Elizabeth 2)

QE2 back in her black hull – with red funnel retained – in 1984. (Tee Adams)

Vistafjord commanded a loyal following. (Bill Miller)

QE2's profile just prior to her 1986/87 refurbishment. This image shows the original funnel and Magrodome open over the Quarter Deck pool. (Cunard/ Michael Gallagher)

▶ **DID YOU KNOW?** ···············

In 1971, QE2 came to the aid of the French ship Antilles, which had run aground off the coast of Mustique.

QE2's steam turbine engines were replaced with diesels, pictured here. (Authors' collection)

Cunard's *Sea Goddess I* and *II* together. (Bill Miller)

Princess Diana aboard *QE2* for a charity cruise. (Cunard/Michael Gallagher)

Margaret Thatcher aboard *QE2* to honour her service during the Falklands. (Cunard/Michael Gallagher)

Queen Elizabeth, the Queen Mother speaks aboard *QE2*. (Cunard/Michael Gallagher)

HM the Queen aboard *QE2* in 1990. (Cunard/Michael Gallagher)

QE2's rendezvous with the Royal Yacht *Britannia*. (Cunard/Michael Gallagher)

Cunard Crown Monarch failed to capture the Australian market. (Bill Miller)

Sagafjord departs on another luxury cruise. (Bill Miller)

Sagafjord off Cayman in 1995. *Sagafjord* was a classic liner with a 5-star rating. (Tee Adams)

In 1994 Cunard acquired the 5-star *Royal Viking Sun*. (Bill Miller)

QE2 passes the World Trade Centre following her 1994 refurbishment. (Cunard/Michael Gallagher)

Nelson Mandela with Captain Warwick aboard *QE2* during his 1998 voyage. (Cunard/Michael Gallagher)

QE2 arriving in Sydney during her 1995 World Cruise. (Cunard/ Michael Gallagher)

QE2 wore the golden lion and speed stripe on her superstructure after her 1994 refit. (Authors' collection)

11

CARNIVAL OWNERSHIP

Our goal is nothing less than to create a new Golden Age of sea travel for those who missed the first.

Cunard president and COO Larry Pimintel on Project Queen Mary

Cunard's fortunes changed dramatically in April 1998. After months of turmoil, the 158-year-old company finally had a buyer in the giant Carnival Corporation. Carnival Corporation had commenced operations as a small cruise line in 1972. The brainchild of American immigrant Ted Arison, the line's approach was to offer fun, cheap cruises departing from US ports such as Miami and Fort Lauderdale.

With a fleet of converted former ocean liners, the early days were turbulent; with the first ship, *Mardi Gras*, running aground during her maiden voyage. However, their business model and marketing position was strong, and Carnival grew to become the dominant player in the youth cruise market. The success of the line allowed it to acquire existing brands. Today the company owns a vast number of cruise ship operators, including P&O Cruises, Costa, Holland America, Seabourn, Princess, Ibero Cruises, AIDA and Cunard.

Despite the size and scale of Carnival, the merchant shipping industry, by and large, were genuinely surprised at the Cunard acquisition. Other lines, such as P&O and Princess (which at the time were not part of Carnival), had looked at Cunard and deemed the company as something of a lost cause. However, Carnival's head, Micky Arison (son of Ted), could see the value in Cunard that no other shipping operator could – the value of its brand.

By late 1998 plans were well underway for the company's transformation, which was enacted the following year. Under the leadership of new president and COO Larry Pimintel, the now Miami-based Cunard set about reinventing itself.

QE2 and *Vistafjord* were both given extensive refurbishments. *QE2*'s refit cost over US$30 million, and included the completion of outstanding interior design work from the 1994 refit, as well as a complete hull strip and repaint back into traditional Cunard colours.

Vistafjord was also treated to an extensive refit, and emerged with a new name – *Caronia*. The name change came with a new feel for the ship, and although *Caronia* retained many of the features that her repeat guests

Far left: Repainted in traditional Cunard livery, QE2 and Caronia shared millennium eve together. (Cunard/Michael Gallagher)

Left: QM2 was built using prefabricated blocks. (Pam Massey)

Far left: The yet-to-be-painted QM2 is taking shape. (Pam Massey)

Left: The name Queen Mary 2 has been attached and is prepared for painting. (Pam Massey)

loved, she was given a very British treatment during the refit. This was a deliberate move, aimed at standardising the Cunard fleet to allow the line to re-establish itself in a niche market.

The remaining vessels in the Cunard fleet – *Royal Viking Sun*, *Sea Goddess I* and *Sea Goddess II* – were transferred into the Carnival-owned Seabourn fleet and renamed *Seabourn Sun*, *Seabourn Goddess I* and *Seabourn Goddess II*. Seabourn had been merged with Cunard in 1998 to form Cunard Line Ltd, a holding company that operated both the Cunard and Seabourn brands. A variety of functions were shared, including websites built off the same design and commonality across brochures and branding.

Further dramatic change for the company occurred on 8 June 1999, when Larry Pimentel announced the company's intention to build the first transatlantic liner since QE2 was launched in 1967. Of the plans, Pimentel told excited reporters that:

The project will lead to development of the heaviest liner ever built; the epitome of elegance, style and grace ... It is our objective to build a new generation of ocean liner that will be the very pinnacle of the shipbuilder's art; the realization of a dream of another time ... Our goal is nothing less than to create a new Golden Age of sea travel for those who missed the first.

QM2 in Southampton for the first time, in December 2003. (Andy Fitzsimmons)

HM the Queen and Commodore R.W. Warwick aboard QM2. (Commodore R.W. Warwick)

QE2 and QM2 in New York. (Thad Constantine)

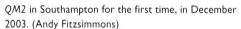

The first official meeting of the planning and design team followed the official announcement. Under the direction of chief naval architect Stephen Payne, the design evolved from a ship of similar dimensions to QE2, to become the longest, largest, tallest, widest and most expensive passenger ship ever built at the time.

There were a variety of reasons why the new liner, codenamed 'Project Queen Mary', was so large. The driving factor for the size was the requirement for a high percentage of balcony accommodation aboard the ship. This was the first ocean liner ever designed with such a requirement and the design team had to think laterally about how this would be achieved, resulting in the creation of sheltered veranda cabins, or 'hull holes', that sat beneath the boat deck.

Other considerations were taken into the design, which added to the ship's bulk. A long streamlined bow, hydrodynamic hull and terraced aft decks were added to the extra space required for the largest ballroom at sea, a full-size planetarium and the magnificent multi-storey Britannia Restaurant.

While much of Cunard's attention was devoted to building their new ship, QE2 and Caronia were enjoying ever-increasing popularity. With the refurbishment work complete, the two ships offered a series of voyages from Southampton, while QE2 maintained her transatlantic schedule. Both vessels celebrated New Year's Eve 1999 off Barbados. Aboard both

Cunarders there was much talk of Project Queen Mary, with particular discussion among passengers and crew over which shipyard would build the new liner, with many traditionalists hoping the work would go to a British yard.

Following a tender process, the French shipyard Chantiers de l'Atlantique was selected to build the new Cunard liner. John Brown, the Scottish yard responsible for the original Queens, had long since shut down, while Harland & Wolff were unsuccessful in their bid for the work. The French shipyard had a pedigree of building ocean liners, having constructed the Normandie and France, as well owning a fitting-out basin and gantry large enough to accommodate the massive new liner. The letter of intent was signed on 10 March 2000, while the formal contracts were signed in November that same year.

The devastating terrorist attacks of 11 September 2001 impacted Cunard; with the QE2 en route to New York at the time of the attacks, the Cunard flagship was diverted to Boston due to the closure of New York. Boston became the default American home for QE2 until she returned to New York in January 2002, making her the first cruise ship to return to the port.

The keel-laying ceremony for Project Queen Mary took place on 4 July 2002. The construction of the new Cunard liner was extremely fast, and only a fraction of the time taken to build the previous Cunard Queens.

This was largely thanks to the adoption of prefabrication in the building process, where large pre-made blocks were assembled to create the finished ship.

So fast was the build that by 22 December 2003 the ship was handed over to Cunard Line. After a shakedown cruise under the command of Commodore Ronald W. Warwick, the ship arrived in Southampton where HM Queen Elizabeth II officially named her *Queen Mary 2* (*QM2*) on 8 January 2004.

On 30 May 2003, Cunard and Saga Holidays announced that Saga had bought *Caronia* with the intention of operating the ship in conjunction with her former fleet mate *Sagafjord*, now *Saga Rose*. Despite the purchase occurring in 2003, *Caronia* remained in the Cunard fleet until late 2004, allowing for a well-patronised farewell season.

That same year, Cunard had announced their intention to build an 80,000-ton cruise ship. To be named *Queen Victoria*, the new vessel's hull was laid down on 12 July 2003 at the Fincanteri yards in Italy. The new vessel was of the 'Vista' class, having originally been allocated to Holland America line.

In January 2004, *QE2* departed on her final world cruise as Cunard's flagship. After a three-month circumnavigation of the globe, the venerable Cunarder rendezvoused with the newer, larger *QM2* in New York, creating much attention. Following a full day side by side, the two Queens departed New York for a tandem transatlantic crossing to Southampton. Upon their arrival, *QM2* officially became flagship of the Cunard fleet.

In mid-2004, Cunard announced that they had transferred ownership of the incomplete *Queen Victoria* to sister-brand P&O Cruises. Renamed *Arcadia*, the vessel was floated out on 26 June 2004 and entered service in March the following year.

The reason for the change was linked to the success of *QM2*. Cunard had identified a niche luxury market for passengers wishing to sail aboard ocean liners, as evidenced by *QM2*'s popularity since her introduction into service as well as the ongoing loyalty of passengers to *QE2* and *Caronia*. To that end, a new *Queen Victoria* was ordered in December 2004 from Fincanteri. Although based on the 'Vista'-class design, the new liner was altered to include some ocean-liner traits. Her bow and forward superstructure was strengthened, allowing her to undertake occasional transatlantic crossings; while the hull was lengthened to create space for a ballroom – a hallmark of previous Cunard Queens. In the words of Cunard Line at the time, the new vessel would 'adhere to the grand ocean liner design inspired by current vessels *QE2* and *QM2*'.

QM2's funnel, based on that aboard QE2, includes a wind scoop at the base to direct smoke away from the aft decks. (Authors' collection)

QM2 is the only ship to have a planetarium. (Authors' collection)

QM2's size is evident in this shot of her at anchor. (Authors' collection)

Left: The *QM2* arrives in Longbeach California. (Nick Souza)

Centre left: *QE2* follows the outbound *QM2* down Southampton Water. (Cunard/ Michael Gallagher)

Bottom left: *QM2* meets *Queen Mary* in Longbeach. (Nick Souza)

Right: *QM2* manoeuvres in the harbour after her rendezvous with the original *Queen Mary* in Longbeach, California. (Nick Souza)

Below: *QE2* with the new *Queen Victoria* at Fort Lauderdale. (Cunard/Michael Gallagher)

Queen Victoria was floated out on 15 January 2007, and entered service with Cunard that December. The ship quickly filled the gap left by Caronia's departure, and introduced a new group of cruisers to Cunard's fleet.

That same year, the Cunard community was shocked at the announcement of QE2's retirement. The 39-year-old liner was enjoying ongoing popularity and it had been widely expected that a proposed refurbishment would keep the liner in service for several years to come. However, this was not to be. Instead, QE2 was sold to Dubai World for a sum of US$100 million. Fortunately for QE2's loyal following there was time to say goodbye, with the official retirement date not until November 2008.

On 13 January 2008, the three Queens met in New York harbour in the first of many celebratory events designed to bid QE2 a farewell, and establish Queen Victoria and QM2 as her successors. This event was followed by a further rendezvous of QE2 and Queen Victoria in Sydney harbour, which mirrored a similar event the previous year when QE2 met QM2 in the Australian city.

In October 2008, QE2 and QM2 undertook a special farewell tandem transatlantic crossing. Travelling both westbound and then eastbound, the event allowed America to say farewell to QE2 for the final time before the ship was retired in November.

With QE2 gone, Cunard continued with plans to create a new Queen Elizabeth. Originally announced in 2007, the new liner was of similar design to Queen Victoria, albeit slightly larger at just over 90,900 tons.

In 2009, Carnival UK opened a new custom-built headquarters in Southampton called Carnival House. With the opening of this building, Cunard's management was relocated into the premises, which also houses a number of other Carnival Corporation brands. In this new working environment, resources between the various brands are shared, with Cunard Line operating in increasingly close ties with P&O.

In late 2010, the new Queen Elizabeth was handed over to Cunard at a ceremony held by the Fincanteri shipyard. Named on 11 October 2010, by HM Queen Elizabeth II, the ship entered service the following day and has since established herself in the Mediterranean cruise market.

Queen Victoria's funnel was also inspired by QE2. (Authors' collection)

ROYAL RENDEZVOUS: QM2 AND QE2 IN SYDNEY

The date 20 February 2007 is one the people of Sydney won't soon forget. On this day the city was brought to a standstill by the meeting of two great ocean liners.

QM2 arrived in Sydney early that morning, making her maiden visit during her inaugural world cruise. The ship, under the command of Captain (now Commodore) Christopher Rynd, performed a 180° manoeuvre near the Sydney Harbour Bridge before docking at the nearby naval base.

During the day, the harbour and surrounding areas became increasingly crowded as people awaited the arrival of QE2. The event had been well marketed, as it was the first time that two Cunard Queens had been together in Sydney since the Second World War.

By the time QE2 arrived in the harbour late that afternoon, a crowd estimated at well over a million people had descended on Sydney. The city was in complete gridlock, with traffic jams lasting well into the night.

QE2 and *Queen Victoria* make for an impressive sight alongside the Sydney Opera House. (Cunard/Michael Gallagher)

QE2 and *Queen Victoria* met in Sydney harbour in 2008. (Cunard/Michael Gallagher)

Bill Miller is a well-known maritime author and lecturer and has had a long affection for the Cunard Line:

As a youngster, watching ships and especially the great liners, in New York harbour, I think the Cunard liners were my favourites. They were the epitome of what great ocean liners were and should be. They were big, immaculate, regal, and capped by those wonderful orange-red & black funnels.

In the 1950s, there might be as many as four Cunard liners in port, at Piers 90 & 92, within a week. Tuesday and Wednesday were, of course, the traditional days for the Queens – one of them was over-nighting in port. And, of course, the Cunard offices in Lower Manhattan, at the bottom end of Broadway in the shipping district, were the grandest. It was, in ways, like visiting a great English country house – there was this extraordinary grandeur.

The Cunard Line was prestige, history, absolute magic in those days – and remain so to this day.

► **DID YOU KNOW?**

QE2 remains the longest-serving express liner in history, travelling more than 5.6 million miles over thirty-nine and a half years.

Far left: *QE2* and *Queen Victoria* rendezvous in Sydney. (Cunard/Michael Gallagher)

Left: *QE2*'s penultimate departure from New York, 2008. (Tee Adams)

The end of an era. The world's most beloved liner docked at Southampton for the last time. (Andy Fitzsimmons)

The legendary *QE2* departs Southampton for ever. (Andy Fitzsimmons)

The morning of 27 November 2008 was the last time that the Red Ensign would fly from *QE2*. (Ross Burnside)

Far left: *QE2* in Dubai at the end of her Cunard career. (Ross Burnside)

Left: Vista Queens: *Queen Victoria* (right) meets *Queen Elizabeth* (left). (Andrew Sassoli-Walker)

12

LOOKING TO THE FUTURE

Our flagship *Queen Mary 2* will recreate history when she sails from Liverpool on 4 July 2015, following in the wake of *Britannia* which left the city 175 years earlier to the day.

Cunard Line on the 175th anniversary celebrations

With the 2010 introduction of the third Cunarder to hold the name *Queen Elizabeth*, the line entered into a new, modern era. The years since Carnival purchased the line have seen Cunard reinvent itself, having replaced all of their tonnage with three new, large ships. Throughout 2011, Cunard marketing boasted the line's position as operating the youngest fleet in the industry.

Earlier that year QM2's popularity had soared following the eruption of Iceland's Eyjafjallajokull volcano. With transatlantic and European aircraft grounded, Cunard's flagship was the only way to travel between Britain and America. A waiting list of over 1,000 people developed for crossings aboard the Cunarder in the weeks following the eruption.

Also during 2011, Cunard announced their intention to re-register their fleet in Hamilton, Bermuda; ending a 171-year tradition of registering their ships in Great Britain. The line had been investigating the concept of weddings at sea for some time; however, legislation relating to the vessels' British registration prohibited this. With the laws in Bermuda more relaxed in regards to marriage at sea, Cunard made the switch commencing with *Queen Elizabeth* on 24 October 2011. *Queen Victoria* followed on 27 October, while QM2's registration was switched on 1 December 2011. The move also saw the vessels' registration letters change, bringing to an end the traditional registration letters of GBTT, which had been used for the original *Queen Mary*, *QE2* and the new *Queen Elizabeth*.

With 2012 marking the 60th anniversary of HM Queen Elizabeth II's coronation, the Cunard fleet was back in the spotlight. The queen has a unique relationship with Cunard, being the only person known to have been present at the launch of all three Cunard ships to carry the name *Queen Elizabeth*.

On 5 June, in a special tribute event, the three Cunarders met in Southampton. With *Queen Elizabeth* and *Queen Victoria* docked, the flagship *QM2* arrived, sailing past her fleet mates carrying a large banner that read 'Congratulations Ma'am'. The event attracted large crowds and a flyover by the RAF's Red Arrows, the first such flyover display in Southampton.

On 27 April 2012, *QM2* welcomed former US President, George H. Bush, and his wife aboard. The couple were taking a transatlantic voyage back to the United States aboard the Cunard flagship. Cunard's president and managing director, Peter Shanks, used the occasion to pay tribute to the line's longest serving senior officer, John Duffy. John Duffy had worked with Cunard for forty-six years, with much of his career aboard *QE2*. With Duffy set to retire, meeting George H. Bush was the latest in a long line of special guests and dignitaries entertained by the hotel manager.

That same year, Cunard celebrated the 5th anniversary of *Queen Victoria*'s entry into service. To mark the occasion, Camilla, Duchess of Cornwall visited the ship she had christened in 2007. The duchess unveiled a portrait of herself, which was hung in the ship's grand lobby. The occasion was also used to mark a milestone in Cunard's relationship with the Princes' Trust charity; with Cunard guests having raised over £800,000.

Cunard has had a long association with Australia and New Zealand, particularly during the World Cruise season. Throughout the 1980s and 1990s, both *QE2* and *Sagafjord* were regular visitors to ports such as Auckland, Sydney and Fremantle.

With three Queens in service, Cunard's presence in the Southern Hemisphere has strengthened, and by 2012 all three Queens had spent time in Australian and New Zealand waters, offering voyages that proved very popular in the local market. In response to this popularity, *QM2* offered an extended circumnavigation of Australia in 2012. The voyage sold out within hours, prompting the line to repeat the schedule in 2014.

Cunard was in the media at the end of 2012; though this time the news centred on a former Cunard ship. *QE2*, which retired to Dubai in 2008 and had been in lay up since arriving in the UAE, hit the headlines when the *Daily Mail* reported that the ship was to be sold for scrap.

The news relating to *QE2* was met by concerned Cunard loyalists, with many taking to Cunard's Facebook page to complain. In early 2013, Cunard confirmed, via their social media channel, that the rumours were untrue, and to this day *QE2* remains in lay up at the Dubai Dry Dock.

For the first three months of 2013, both *QM2* and *Queen Victoria* were deployed on the annual world cruise. *Queen Victoria* undertook a westbound voyage, taking in ports along the west coast of the US before heading across the Pacific, while *QM2* sailed eastbound, via Suez and Asia, to Australia. *QM2*'s voyage included an extended circumnavigation of New Zealand, which saw the 151,400-ton liner visit Milford Sound for the first time.

Queen Victoria and *Queen Elizabeth* (foreground) together in Fort Lauderdale. (Cunard/Michael Gallagher)

Queen Elizabeth departing Fort Lauderdale for the first time. (Cunard/Michael Gallagher)

In July *QM2* completed her 200th transatlantic crossing. The eastbound voyage was well subscribed, having sold out months in advance, and included an array of special guests.

The year ended on a happy note, with Cunard announcing further details of the 175th anniversary celebrations being prepared for 2015. In the first months of 2014, tickets for a variety of celebratory cruises went on sale. These sailings included a commemorative voyage aboard *Queen Victoria* for the 100th anniversary of the sinking of *Lusitania*; a transatlantic crossing from Liverpool to Boston aboard *QM2*; and the meeting of the three Queens in Liverpool.

Cunard celebrated the 10th anniversary of *QM2* in 2014 with a series of special events. During her annual world cruise, the ship made a number of maiden calls to celebrate her decade in service, while the three Cunarders met in both Lisbon and Southampton to mark the anniversary; drawing large crowds and reinforcing the popularity of Cunard.

As Cunard enters its 175th year, the brand enjoys soaring popularity. Few other lines offer voyages that sell out within minutes of going on sale. The passengers who revisit Cunard ships over and over again, along with the crew who serve aboard the current fleet, are creating the future history of this line.

Here's to the future of the Cunard Line.

Vistas at sea: Queens *Elizabeth* and *Victoria*. (Cunard/Michael Gallagher)

Above and Right: *QM2*'s immense size is evident in these images of the liner at anchor off Monte Carlo. (Authors' collection)

‘ **Christel Hansen is well known as the captain's secretary aboard *QM2*; however, she started her career aboard *Vistafjord*:**

Vistafjord was a very homely and friendly ship, a really nice atmosphere. It was the perfect size – 700 passengers and 350 crew – and had very good itineraries (including three days in Sydney on one occasion).

Most passengers came back again and again. We all were one big family. Those that know each other from back then (both passengers and crew) still have a special connection and so many good memories to share.

I don't think I would have stayed at sea to begin with if it wasn't because I was on *Vistafjord*. It was silver service, true 5-star. It was a home away from home. ’

Left: *QM2* seen in Gibraltar at close quarters with *Independence of the Seas*. (Authors' collection)

Below: Accommodation aboard *Queen Victoria* is modern and spacious. (Authors' collection)

Far Left: *Queen Elizabeth* all lit up at night. (Cunard/Michael Gallagher)

Left: *Queen Victoria* near the New York skyscrapers. (Cunard/Michael Gallagher)

Below left: *QM2* near the Statue of Liberty. (Cunard/Michael Gallagher)

Below right: The three Queens, *Elizabeth*, *Victoria* and *Mary 2*. (Cunard/Michael Gallagher)

▶ **DID YOU KNOW?**

The iconic Cunard Building in Liverpool is being converted into a cruise terminal.

Above and Right: *Queen Victoria* at anchor at the UNESCO-protected Geirangerfjord, Norway. (Authors' collection)

Cunard's three modern Queens in New York. (Cunard/Michael Gallagher)

▶ DID YOU KNOW?

In 2013, QM2 came to the aid of rower Mylène Paquette, who got into difficulty whilst attempting to row solo across the Atlantic.

QE2 heading out to sea after her maiden and only call at Albany, Western Australia. (Jan Frame)

AFTERWORD

by Ann Sherry, AO, Carnival Australia, CEO

I am delighted to have this opportunity to congratulate Cunard Line on its 175th anniversary and on its contemporary reputation as one of the world's most distinctive luxury cruise brands.

Cunard's current fleet – flagship *Queen Mary 2*, *Queen Victoria* and *Queen Elizabeth* – continue a powerful Cunard connection with Australia and New Zealand that covers much of the line's heritage.

Over the years, Australians and New Zealanders have taken the three Cunard Queens to their hearts and look forward each year with anticipation to their world voyage visits.

Queen Mary 2 has the distinction of having brought Sydney to a standstill on her maiden visit in 2007 and recent years, when *Queen Mary 2* has spent extended periods here, we have truly felt a certain kinship that she is indeed 'our' ship as well.

In the same way, prior to the current fleet, *QE2* was our Cunard link to the golden age of sailing aboard grand ocean liners.

For many Australian and New Zealand families, there is also a very strong emotional link to Cunard Line. Thousands of Australian soldiers, airmen and nurses sailed to war on the original *Queen Mary* and *Queen Elizabeth*, when both were called up for service in the Second World War as troopships.

In 2011, Carnival Australia was privileged to invite fifty of the veterans who sailed on the two Cunard ships to a special remembrance service on board *Queen Mary 2* and a lunch in the Britannia Restaurant dedicated to these members of 'Australia's Finest Generation'.

QM2 and *Queen Victoria* photographed from *Queen Elizabeth* during the Three Queens Diamond Jubilee Rendezvous. (Robyn Burn)

In recent years, as a new generation has discovered cruising as a wonderful holiday experience, Cunard Line has played a part in generating the sense of excitement that has made Australia and New Zealand one of the world's fastest-growing cruise markets.

Today, Cunard Line, with its magnificent ships and impeccable White Star service, carries forward the distinguished and unparalleled heritage of a brand synonymous with luxury cruising at its best.

I have no doubt that Cunard will enjoy continued success as many more Australians and New Zealanders realise their dream of sailing with a shipping line that has become so much a part of our own heritage and contemporary cruise choices.

Ann Sherry, AO,
Chief Executive Officer, Carnival Australia

QE2 berthed at Albany during her farewell world cruise. (Authors' collection)

BIBLIOGRAPHY

Books and Articles

Braynard, F.O. and Miller, W.H., *Picture History of the Cunard Line* (Dover; United Kingdom, 1991).

Britton, A., *RMS Mauretania* (The History Press; United Kingdom, 2013).

Chirnside, M., *Aquitania: The Ship Beautiful* (The History Press; United Kingdom, 2009).

De Kerbrech, R., *Ships of the White Star Line* (Ian Allen Publishing; United Kingdom, 2009).

Dickens, C., *American Notes: John W. Lovell & Co.* (New York; United States, 1842). Source: Archive.org.

Frame, C. and Cross, R., *The Evolution of the Transatlantic Liner* (The History Press; United Kingdom, 2013).

Frame, C. and Cross, R., *The Cunard Story* (The History Press; United Kingdom, 2010).

Frame, C. and Cross, R., *The QE2 Story* (The History Press; United Kingdom, 2009).

Gandy, M., 'The Britannia Cup', *The Antiques Magazine*, Vol. 122 (July 1982), pp. 156–8.

Grant, R.G., *Flight: The Complete History* (Dorling Kindersley Limited; United Kingdom, 2007).

Harding, S. Gray, *Ghost: The RMS Queen Mary at War* (Pictorial Histories Publishing Company; United States of America, 1982).

Harvey, C. and Cartwright, R., *The Saga Sisters* (The History Press; United Kingdom, 2006).

Hutchings, D.F., *RMS Queen Elizabeth – From Victory to Valhalla* (Kingfisher Publications; United Kingdom, 1990).

Langley, J.G., *Steam Lion: A Biography of Samuel Cunard* (Brick Tower Press; United States of America, 2006).

Maxtone-Graham, J. and Lloyd, H., *Queen Mary 2: The Greatest Ocean Liner of Our Time* (Bulfinch; United Kingdom, 2004).

McCutcheon, J., *Cunard: A Photographic History* (Tempus; United Kingdom, 2004).

Miller, W.H., *Pictorial Encyclopedia of Ocean Liners 1860–1994* (Dover; United Kingdom, 1995).

Miller, W.H., *Picture History of British Ocean Liners: 1900 to the Present* (Dover; United Kingdom, 2001).

Miller, W.H., *Picture History of the Queen Mary and Queen Elizabeth* (Dover; United Kingdom, 2001).

Miller, W.H., SS *United States: Speed Queen of the Seas* (Amberley Publishing; United Kingdom, 2010).

Osborne, B.D. and Armstrong, R., *Scotland's Greatest Ships* (Luthan Press Ltd; United Kingdom, 2007).

Plisson, P., *Queen Mary 2: The Birth of a Legend: Harry. N* (Abrams; United Kingdom, 2004).

Warwick, R.W., *QE2: The Cunard Line Flagship Queen Elizabeth II* (Norton; United Kingdom, 1999).

Warwick, S. and Roussel, M., *Shipwrecks of the Cunard Line* (The History Press; United Kingdom, 2012).

Williams, D., *Cunard's Legendary Queens of the Seas* (Ian Allen Publishing; United Kingdom, 2004).

Wills, E., *The Fleet, 1840–2004: Cunard's Floating Palaces from the Earliest Days of Steam to Queen Mary 2* (The Open Agency; United Kingdom, 2004).

Film

Queen Mary Launch, c. 1934.

Queen Elizabeth Launch, c. 1939.

The Great Ships television series, various episodes (Perpetual Motion Films).

The Liners television series, various episodes (Demand DVD).

Personal Conversations

Commodore R.W. Warwick.
Commodore C. Rynd.
Commodore J. Burton-Hall.
Captain I. McNaught.
Cunard Line Official Historian, M. Gallagher.

Company Documents

Cunard Line, On-board Promotional Material (various versions), 2009.
Cunard Line, *Queen Mary 2: Technical and Bridge Facts* (Various Versions), 2009.

Websites (General)

Chris' Cunard Page: www.chriscunard.com
Cunard's Official Website: www.cunard.com

Websites (Specific)

Archives Today: http://archive.today – Navies in Transition. Accessed 19 July 2014.
Clydesite: www.clydesite.co.uk – Cunard Cargo Ship Database at Clydesite.
Genealogy website: http://rmhh.co.uk – RMS *Andria* pages at Hall Genealogy website.
The Lusitania Resource: www.rmslusitania.info – *Lusitania* in the war.
Marconi Website: www.marconigraph.com – Includes historical notes.
Rob Lightbody's *QE2* website: www.roblightbody.com – *Queen Elizabeth 2*.
Daily Mail: www.dailymail.co.uk – 'End of an Era as Iconic QE2 sold for scrap'. Accessed 20/06/2014.
Source News: www.soue.org.uk – *Turbinia* information.

Newspapers

Author unknown, 'Takeover offer for Cunard planned by Trafalgar House', *Montreal Gazette*, 2 July 1971.
Author unknown, 'Cunard Chief Resigns', *Herald Scotland*, 21 September 1996.
Cowell, A., 'Belfast Shipyard Loses Bid to Build *Queen Mary 2*, and Many Jobs', *New York Times*, 11 March 2000.
Granger Blair, W., 'B.O.A.C. buys out Cunard's share; $32.2-Million price to help ship line offset losses', *The New York Times*, 16 September 1966, pp. 55.
Ipsen, E., 'Kværner is Close to Bidding for Troubled Group: Lifeline for Trafalgar House?', *The New York Times*, 28 February 1996.
Jones, S., 'QE2 sold to become Floating Hotel', *Travel Weekly*, 18 June 2007.
McDowell, E., 'Chief's Strategy for Ailing Cruise Line', *The New York Times*, 6 August 1996.

For Further Reading

If you're interested in the history of other ocean liners written by Chris Frame and Rachelle Cross, read:

The Evolution of the Transatlantic Liner.
The QM2 Story.
The QE2 Story.

QM2: A Photographic Journey.
QE2: A Photographic Journey.
Queen Victoria: A Photographic Journey.
Queen Elizabeth: A Photographic Journey.

If you're interested in the history of P&O:

Henderson, Rob, Cremer, Doug, Frame, Chris and Cross, Rachelle, *A Photographic of P&O Cruises.*

Photographic/Bibliographical Notice

All images used within this book are reproduced with the express permission of the photograph/collection owner. All images are referenced as such. Copyright and ownership of the images remain with the photograph owner/collection owner/photographer.

Every effort has been made to reference information correctly. Where information was found digitally, every effort was made to reference the original source.

Any bibliographic errors or omissions will be remedied in future editions.